Vintage Wein

Vintage

A SHAAR PRESS PUBLICATION

The collected wit and wisdom,
the choicest anecdotes and vignettes of
RABBI BEREL WEIN

---

by Dr. James David Weiss

© *Copyright 1992 by* Dr. James David Weiss and Shaar Press

First edition — First Impression / October 1992

ALL RIGHTS RESERVED

No part of this book may be reproduced **in any form,** *photocopy, electronic media, or otherwise without* **written** *permission from the copyright holder, except by a reviewer who wishes to quote brief passages in connection with a review written for inclusion in magazines or newspapers.*

THE RIGHTS OF THE COPYRIGHT HOLDER WILL BE STRICTLY ENFORCED.

Cover simulated from photo of Rabbi Wein.
Photo by Martin Ginsberg

Published by **SHAAR PRESS**
Distributed by **MESORAH PUBLICATIONS, LTD.**
4401 Second Avenue / Brooklyn, New York 11232 / (718) 921-9000

Distributed in Israel by J. GROSSMAN
Rechov Harav Uziel 117 / Jerusalem, Israel

Distributed in Europe by J. LEHMANN HEBREW BOOKSELLERS
20 Cambridge Terrace / Gateshead, Tyne and Wear / England NE8 1RP

Distributed in Australia and New Zealand by GOLD'S BOOK & GIFT SHOP
36 William Street / Balaclava 3183, Vic., Australia

Distributed in South Africa by KOLLEL BOOKSHOP
22 Muller Street / Yeoville 2198 / Johannesburg, South Africa

ISBN: 0-89906-598-8 Hard Cover
ISBN: 0-89906-599-6 Paperback

Printed in the United States of America by Noble Book Press
Custom bound by Sefercraft, Inc. / 4401 Second Avenue / Brooklyn, N.Y. 11232

To

Hill Krakovsky, *z'l*,

my beloved father-in-law,

who always enjoyed listening

to a good story

Table of Contents

Foreword by Rabbi Berel Wein	15
Author's Preface	19
Acknowledgments	21
Author's Introduction	23

1 On the Road Again — 33

Stretch Limo	35
Asleep at the Wheel	37
On the Road Again	39
The Jewish History Tapes	39
Reserved	41
L'shaim Shamayim	44
The Chanukah Clock	46
Saddam and Me	48
The Big Joke	50
The Rabbi and the Priest	51

2 Food for Thought — 57

Chocolate Bar	59
Und Vos Zugt Gott?	62
Bow-U	66
Tzitzis	66
The Humane Society Strikes Again	70
Food, Glorious Food	72

3 Kosher Money — 77

The Slap Heard Round the World	80
We Don't Believe in Ourselves	81
Unexpected Profits	83
The Law of Increasing Returns	84

Hefsed Merubah	84
Trump Cards	86
If I Were a Rich Man	88
If I Were a Rich Man #2	89
Liquid Assets	91
Achdüs Yisroel	93
Tremendous Opportunities	94
Rabbi Kaplan, the Wine Maker	95
Family Business	96
Warm Hands	97
The Story of Two Wills	98
The $28,000 Coffin	102

4 An Immortal People — 109

Comrade Yaakov	111
Prisoners of Zion and their Dreams	111
Mendelevitch, the Refusenik	113
Trotsky's Grandson	114
Pesach in Chernobyl	115
Generation Gap	118
The Disco Rabbi	121
Shomair Hatzair	123
Yossel the *Mohel*	124
The Mexican-American Traffic Cop	125
Talmid "Kokom"	126
A *Baal Teshuvah* Story	129

5 The Song of a Yeshiva — 137

Boys Town	139
Rabbi Mendel Kaplan	140
Rabbi Kaplan Shorts	143
Non-Conformists	144
In the Beginning	145
Essay Contest	147

Yeshiva Lunchrooms	149
Snow Days	151
Abraham Lincoln's Drawer	151
Vocational Guidance	154
Satisfaction Guaranteed	155
The *Sura Yeshiva*	157
God's Sense of Humor	157
Kovod	158
The Odd Couple	160

6 Israel and the Holocaust — 167

Mama	168
Yad Vashem	172
Emperor Hadrian	174
Persians and Nazis	175
Herzl and the Kaiser	177
One More Generation	179
Private Benjamin	180
Stepping Out	181
Arab Zionists	181
Miracles	182
The Sale	183
The 1929 Riots	183
Halleluyah	184

7 Golus in America — 189

Finnish Lumber	192
Rights of First Refusal	193
Golus in America	194
The Jewish Problem	197
Polarization	198
Pluralism	199
Esrog and *Lulav*	201
Yuppie Wein	203

Golus Shorts	204
Four Wise Men	205
Rabbi Wein's Grandfather	206

8 Rabbis and the Rabbinate — 213

Rabbi Wein's Father-in-Law	216
Shortest Speech Ever Made by a Rabbi	218
Rabbi Meir's Back	218
Frumkeit	219
Word of Mouth	222
Reb Yaakov	224
The Smile of an Orphan	226
Educational Planning	229
The Game of Marbles	230
Lo Sikom	231
The *Nazir*	232
Like Father-in-Law Like Son-in-Law	235
The Truth Consoles	236
A Grobbe Taus	239
Sayings of the *Kotzker*	240
A Good Memory	242
The Revenge on the *Tzaddik*	242
The Satmar Rav and the Butcher	243
Rabbi Wein Stories Told on Himself	246
The Handkerchief	248
Clarity	249
Sophistication	250
The Rabbinate . . . or What's Left of it	251
The Rabbi Goes on Strike	252
The $150,000 Rabbi	253

9 The Mussar Shmooze — 257

The Main Task in Life	258
The Butcher's Complaint	261

Leitzonis	264
It's No Trick	265
The Oldest Jew	267
Tikkun	270
Vintage Wein	270
Three-Ring Circus	271
Fish Paper	272
Sportorama	273
The Acquisitive Desire	275
Simplicity	276
Naivete	278
Forest Lawn	279
Shmeck Taback	279
The Last Rabbi Wein Story	283

Foreword

by Rabbi Berel Wein

Dr. James Weiss is an old and dear friend of mine. He has heard me speak hundreds of times and yet he remains a friend of mine. He also has an ear for conversation, sense for anecdotes and a facile pen. I am therefore flattered that he has devoted a number of years of his life to write this book. In it, through anecdotes, stories, parables and relatively few words of wisdom, he has captured the essence of much of my life experience and outlook on people, events and the foibles of human existence.

The book, which I have read a number of times, also has served to give me a clearer sense of identity. I now am able to see myself as others see and hear me. This may not always be flattering, and is always most surprising, but on the whole I feel it to be worthwhile and instructive. Many times in life we do not respond to our true name and self because we are confused as to our true identity. Which leads me to tell you a story about myself.

Once I was traveling from Newark Airport to Lincoln, Nebraska via Chicago's O'Hare Airport. My plane was to depart at 8:30 A.M. and arrive in Chicago for a noon connection to Lincoln. I left my home at 6:30 A.M. but ran into the first snow storm of the winter which tied up traffic and did not allow me to reach Newark until 9:00 A.M. Frustrated and irritated, I told my tale of woe to the ticket agent who promptly and cheerily booked me on the 10:00 A.M. flight to Chicago and the 1:00 P.M. connection to Lincoln, I remarked to her that I had ordered a kosher meal on my earlier flights and asked if she could arrange the same on my new flights. She told me that, even though she would type my request into the computer, there was probably not enough time to have the meals on board my flights.

After entering the airplane, finding my seat and seating myself comfortably, the stewardess approached me and noticing my yarmulke asked me if I had ordered a special meal. I recounted my whole story to her — how I missed my original plane and had ordered a kosher meal for this flight only a few minutes before — and asked her if perhaps they had my meal on board. After checking the galley she told me that there was one kosher meal on board but it was not for Wein but rather for Lesh. I countered that poor Mr. Lesh was probably also stuck in traffic and perhaps missed the plane. She promptly announced on the loud speaker that Mr. Lesh should please identify himself. When no one responded, the stewardess smilingly presented me with the kosher meal and also gleefully informed me that according to her manifest, Mr. Lesh was scheduled to be on my connection to Lincoln and therefore I should have no trouble having a kosher lunch on my flight to Lincoln. When I sat down in my seat on my connecting flight to Lincoln I was convinced that I would have a kosher meal awaiting me. As the flight attendant approached me and asked for my name I almost nonchalantly told her "I believe there is a kosher meal aboard for Mr. Lesh." She smiled, returned to the galley and then came back to me and said apologetically, "I'm sorry, the only kosher meal aboard is for someone named Wein." Hunger pains forced me to think quickly, I said to her, "Why don't you ask if Wein is on the plane?" She announced on the public address system a request that Mr. Wein identify himself. Since no one responded to her request, she graciously gave me Wein's kosher meal. Just desserts!

Many times in life one does not respond to one's real name, calling and destiny. The Lord however usually conspires to present us with situations in life that cause us to look inwardly and identify ourselves honestly. He also provides us with a mirror from the outside world to help us know what values we represent to others and how they view us. This book is therefore a humbling and simultaneously uplifting experience for me. I hope that it will be an enjoyable and educational one for you.

Author's Preface

Rabbi Berel Wein wears many hats — all black. He is a distinguished Torah scholar, author of works of Talmudic commentary and responsa, the founder of Yeshiva Shaarei Torah, Rav of Bais Torah synagogue in Monsey, author of *Triumph of Survival: The Story of the Jews in the Modern Era* (Shaar Press), a member of the Illinois Bar, a former Director of the O.U. (Union of Orthodox Jewish Congregations of America), and the creator of a most wonderful series of Jewish history tapes. He is a consummate and dedicated teacher of the Talmud and Codes; frequently he returns from a far-off speaking engagement and goes directly from the airport to the study hall to deliver his complex lecture, without missing a beat. But his most important role to the broad Jewish public is the least pretentious and probably the one he does best — speaking to groups of people about what it means to be a Jew.

In simple, eloquent speeches, he has made Jews around the world proud to be Jews. His sentences soar with majesty and give his listeners comfort and direction in these disturbing times. In an effort to spread his message, I have written a book about what I feel is the cornerstone of his talent — the "Rabbi Wein story," that special blend of incident and insight that illuminates our world for us.

However, converting a spoken experience into a textual one has not been without its problems. Rabbi Wein's dry, midwestern delivery will carry a joke forward even when its content value is weak. How does a writer capture that doughty South Chicago accent? How does one pause in print the way the Rabbi can in mid-lecture, gazing down from the pulpit at his listeners? There are no word processors with a Lithuanian soul.

Furthermore, capturing the authentic version of a Rabbi Wein anecdote is a difficult task because he tailors his speeches to suit the tastes of his audiences. One day in Monsey, for instance, he spoke at a Shvut Ami breakfast meeting for Russian Jewry, a Torah U'Mesorah (National Society for Hebrew Day Schools) fundraising brunch later that morning and a Kupath Ezra (Charity Fund) parlor meeting in the early evening. I was at the three Monsey fundraisers and he used the same topical vignette to introduce his talks, but shaded the story each time to meet the needs of the audience of the moment. By the evening speech, the third time around that day, I thought I knew where the laughs were coming, but he fooled me nonetheless.

Keeping these issues of tone and content in mind, I hope I deliver enough of the real man to encourage you to learn more about his vision of the world of Torah. "Rumors to the contrary notwithstanding" — to employ one of Rabbi Wein's hallmark expressions — I do not claim infallibility. Therefore, I take full responsibility for inaccuracies, or infelicites in tone and fact. Blame me for any errors in taste or judgment. Rabbi Wein is the soul of refinement and good sense, and would not harm anyone.

Acknowledgments

First and foremost let me thank Yisroel Epstein who is responsible for at least twenty of the best stories. He is a most talented writer who was able to remember the anecdotes of his Rebbe and write them with inspiring skill. Converting what was spoken into written form was a daunting task, but Yisroel set an example that was instructive. I owe him much, for he is also a crackerjack editor who taught me the meaning of "writer's embellishment." Without his gifted "red pencil" you would be reading a lot more than you needed to. Sruli did not permit me to put his name on the cover, but his assistance was vital to the outcome of this effort and this book was a collaborative effort.

I've only been a member of Bais Torah for six years so in order to resurrect the stories told before my time I've asked people to recall their favorite Rabbi Wein story. Chief memory aids were: Rabbi Yaakov Hain, Dr. David Kaplan, Daniel Hirsch and Rabbi Chaim Z. Levitan; may their data banks function at high levels for many more vignettes.

For straightening out my word processing muddles, I am especially indebted to Avi Gittler. His wizardry will be long remembered. Thanks also to Betty Sinowitz and Joshua Kaplan who helped me track down and tame the "binary beast."

For this undertaking, I was ably guided by Yaakov Astor, who, with his unfailing good humor and flair for creative problem solving, coordinated many of the myriad facets that went into publishing this book. Yaakov shaped this book and also gave it its title and I'm grateful to have worked with him.

What acknowledgment section would be complete without mentioning the writer's family. In my case, though, this is more than customary gratitude — my family provided substantial writing support. My sons, Rabbi Moishe, and Daniel, were of enormous editorial assistance as the publication deadline approached. Their insights into writing helped me make intelligent and tasteful decisions. I thank Hashem for giving me sons who are devoted *talmidei chachamim* and who are such gifted arbiters of English usage. They taught me a lot. Appreciation must also go to Herman, my son, who believed in the project from the beginning and brought over my granddaughter, Naomi, whenever I needed spiritual uplift.

Warmest thanks for going above and beyond to the dedicated staff at Shaar Press: Eli Kroen, Mrs. Ethel Gottlieb, Mrs. Chavie Friedman, Nichie Feendrich, Mindy Kohn and all the other unsung heroes.

A special acknowledgment and heartfelt thanks I give to my wife, Joanna, for overseeing the whole editorial process and supporting me significantly in every phase of writing this book. Hashem has blessed me with a fine, loving wife who is also a naturally gifted writer and a sharp, keen critic. May I some day be worthy of her and help her with her book.

I acknowledge the whole Bais Torah and Shaarei Torah family especially Dr. and Mrs. David Hammer for nurturing this project and helping it succeed. And, finally, I thank Rabbi Wein for being Rabbi Wein.

Hashem has been exceptionally kind and generous to my family. I don't know where we all would be without His bountiful gifts.

Dr. James Weiss

Author's Introduction

Twenty-four years ago, when my wife and I moved to Monsey, neither of us were observant Jews. After a few years, my wife started attending a local Orthodox synagogue, headed by Rabbi Berel Wein, and not too long afterwards she became a *Shomeres Shabbos* (Sabbath observer).

For my part, I was a die-hard secular humanist who did not believe in anything except the right of someone to believe in anything one felt was important. That right I would defend vigorously. My wife's decision to become observant forced me to practice what I preached. Reluctantly, I went along with her spiritual endeavors. I respected *Shabbos* and *Yom Tov* and tried not to contaminate her kitchen.

However, in spite of good intentions, there were rough moments. Two-day holidays were always an ordeal for me. Yet, attending Passover Seders at the beloved Beckers and Katzes, our neighbors, eased the difficult times. We observed the holidays as a family even though we did not believe as one family. Eventually, though, I became inured. I only set down one rule: "No *shaitels*." (My wife, Joanna, went along with my dictum in the beginning, but now I have relented and today she has a collection of *shaitels,* 'wigs.')

Slowly I was affected by my wife's piety and became more observant. She would return from synagogue on *Shabbos* and share with me many of her Rabbi's speeches. The stories took place in airplanes or bus stops, animal game farms, Norwegian fjords, Bronx catering halls — even for a world traveler, this was an unusual mixture of sites. The exotic and contrived stories — the ones that could never have happened — caught my fancy. I loved the stories because they were so improbable — this Rabbi really got around.

On *Shabbos,* when I got back from golf, my wife, would regale me with another Rabbi Wein story and in return I would tell her my golf story. Both were legends, but mine, I had to admit, paled beside the Rabbi's. After about a year of this Sabbath routine, for some inexplicable reason, Joanna began to forget the punchlines of the Rabbi's stories. She would just forget the climax. Nothing could induce her to remember the last line, and it irritated me no end.

"Why can't you remember?" I complained to her. Finally, I issued an ultimatum. "Either remember the whole story, or don't tell it."

So she kept mum. Every Saturday we knew she had a Rabbi Wein story to tell but she kept quiet. This was an intolerable situation because I knew when she came home she had heard some great stories, especially when the Rabbi returned from an overseas jaunt. So one day, about seven years ago, I came home from golf early, showered, changed my clothes, and went to hear Rabbi Wein deliver his *Shabbos Hagodol* (Sabbath before Passover) sermon at four in the afternoon at Bais Torah Synagogue.

I found a seat in the back and listened carefully as the sermon went on for an hour. For some reason, the speech did not contain a single joke. I learned later that on *Shabbos Hagodol* jokes were inappropriate. Rabbi Wein lectured on the principle of what constitutes a *shiur,* the minimum quantity of *matzah* one must eat Passover night. I was floored; there was not a joke or a "Rabbi Wein story" in the whole speech — just straight Talmud. But what a speech it was! I can't remember the conclusion, but I knew I had been taken on a fascinating intellectual trip. It was the most "serious" fun I had since listening to Adlai Stevenson speak to the American public during his ill-fated presidential campaign.

What an exciting mind was functioning at the pulpit! What an outstanding orator he was! After that *Shabbos,* I returned to synagogue again and again to hear the man speak. He had an inexhaustible supply of illuminating stories, selected from all spheres of human activity and from all centuries. Hellenism, international date lines, brain death, and the futility of the Chicago Cubs — seemingly nothing in life past or present was beyond his reach. His world view was austere and spiritual but he had a winsome and captivating style. As one of his congregants said to me later, "In every speech he will say something that is very endearing."

In short, my journey to Orthodox Judaism was ignited by the oratory of Rabbi Wein. He offered me a different view of traditional observance. It was a perspective so compelling and enriching that I could not ignore it.

In the yeshivas I went to as a child, Rabbis never seemed to be talking to me. I felt as if I had nothing in common with them. My parents, even though they were not observant, enrolled me in the RJJ Yeshiva (Rabbi Jacob Joseph, 165-7 Henry Street on the lower East Side of New York City) to keep me safely occupied and off the streets while they worked. I didn't even own a pair of *tzitzis* and the Rabbis were at a loss as to how to deal with me and my "unorthodox" behavior.

Rabbi Wein, on the other hand, was talking directly to me. He spoke about being Jewish with cogency and charm. For me, he was Isaiah and Moses and every great Jew who spoke truthfully about Jewish destiny. His was an exalted vision that I wanted to share. I remember thinking to myself that if I had had a Rabbi like him when I went to yeshiva I probably would still be there.

Yet, I held back from committing to *halachic* Judaism. After about two years of listening to him on *Shabbos* and learning a little during the week in his classes, I was still only dipping my toe in the sea of Torah.

That summer, my wife and I took a trip to *Eretz Yisroel*. Part of the trip included touring the religious community of Bnei Brak and visiting the Ponevezher Yeshiva. When he was a rabbi in Miami, Rabbi Wein would drive Rav Kahaneman, the Ponevezher Rav, to wealthy citizens to raise funds for his yeshiva. I had heard Rabbi Wein tell many stories about Rav Kahaneman. In fact, I heard so many of these stories that I felt I knew the Rav personally. On the eve of our departure for Israel, I told Rabbi Wein that I planned to visit the Ponevezher Yeshiva and if the Rav was going to be there I would give him Rabbi Wein's regards. Rabbi Wein gave me his most enigmatic Lithuanian smile and said, "Go right ahead."

We arrived in Bnei Brak at ten o'clock in the morning. I remembered our tour guide informed us that although there were tens of thousands of people living there, the city had no jail and little violent crime. This was one of those striking details that fascinated me about the Land of Israel. Three weeks in Israel were having their effect — I was touched in many ways by the beauty of my heritage.

After walking about the streets of Bnei Brak for a half hour, we were taken to the *bais medresh* (study hall) of the Ponevezher Yeshiva. Inside we were shown the famous Holy Ark that was imported from Europe — golden carvings adorned its massive front. Giant ceiling fans, hanging from chains forty feet overhead, turned lazily. Five hundred students, boys and young men, all dressed in white shirts and black pants, were learning the Talmud. As I walked the aisles I was impressed by the decorum in the tumult of the learning. A strange, noisy serenity prevailed in the hall.

I wanted to deliver Rabbi Wein's message to Rav Kahaneman. I knew a little Yiddish so I kept asking students, *"Vo ist der Ponevezher Rav?"* and they looked at me quizzically and waved me to the back of the hall. I searched in vain; all I saw were hundreds of white-shirted Talmud scholars. Then, drifting near one densely packed cluster, I thought I struck gold. There, a bigger than usual group was hunched over a figure, and I heard one boy announce that the Rav was answering questions. I approached and had to peel off about six boys to get a glimpse at the central figure. A small white-bearded Rabbi was holding forth, a tiny, aged man in a large pill-box *yarmulke*. The boys were pressed close to him, hanging on his every word, inches away from his waxy, almost blue-tinted face.

I waited for a break in the learning and then said, *"Ich breng a gruss fun America, fun Rav Wein."* ("I bring a greeting from Rabbi Wein in America.")

"Ich ken nisht Rabbi Wein." ("I don't know Rabbi Wein.")

He was about to turn away when he did a double take and looked into my eyes, *"Aber, du — du bist a Yid?"* ("But you, are you Jewish?") he asked, pointing a finger at me in kindly, hopeful accusation.

I assured him I was, *"Avadah, avadah geviss."* ("Of course, of course I am.") *"Ich breng dir a gruss fun Rav Wein in Monsey. Du kanst em fun Miami."* ("I bring you greetings from Rabbi Wein; you knew him in Miami.")

"Ich hab dir gezugt ich ken em nisht, du meinst Rav Kahaneman — ich bin Rav Shach und ich bin keinmal nit gevain in Miami." ("I told you already I don't know him — you must mean Rav Kahaneman. I'm Rav Shach and I have never been to Miami.")

He broke off our meeting with a soft piece of advice: *"Aber gedenk, der ikkar zach mit a yid iz tzu zain shomer Shabbos. Dos iz der ikker zach."* ("But remember, the most important issue for a Jew is to be a Sabbath observer.") He smiled at me most kindly, wagged his finger admonishingly, and then gave me a blessing, *"Zolst du zein a gebentshte Yid."* ("You should be a blessed Jew.")

The abruptness with which he blessed me, and the accuracy with which he immediately assessed my level of observance left me speechless. How did he know who I was and where I was holding?

One of the points Rabbi Wein frequently stresses is the idea that we may think we're doing something for one reason, but, in truth, God is sending us out to accomplish His own entirely different goal. I had thought Rav Shach was Rav Kahaneman, the last Ponevezher Rav, who had died many years before, in 1969 — yet even though I did not know who Rav Shach was, he seemed to know all about me. Although 93 at the time, he still had a penetrating intelligence and used it to size me up, fearlessly but gently telling me the truth about myself. I could not be a Jew without *Shabbos* — that was the covenantal truth.

So, there I was thinking I was bringing greetings to a famous Rabbi from a trusted friend. It turned out that neither had ever met the other but both of them had my number. In the end, I was the one who got the message. I left Bnei Brak that summer an unsettled man and before the *Yomim Tovim* arrived that important year I decided to beome *Shomer Shabbos*.

Once, five years ago, I went to Bais Torah to hear vignettes and amusing stories; what I received instead was a glimpse of the beauty and grandeur of a Torah way of life. Now, I eagerly go to Bais Torah and wait for the Rabbi to return from his excursions into the world, to renew my spirits with more stories about Jews and Jewish destiny — "those that have occurred and those that are going to happen."

Vintage Wein

1
On the Road Again

Near the end of his life, Rabbi Shamshon Raphael Hirsch announced that he was going to tour Switzerland on foot. His disciples were alarmed and tried to dissuade him from risking his health. Rabbi Hirsch explained to them, "When I come before the Almighty, I will have to answer for many things. But what will I tell Him when He asks me, 'Shamshon, did you see My Alps?'"

On the Road Again

t once came to pass that Rabbi Wein had driven into Manhattan for an appointment with a generous benefactor of the yeshiva. He surveyed the streets in search of a parking spot and was happy to have found one just two blocks from his destination. He parked his car and walked uptown to his friend's

office. However, on the way he noticed that every parked car ahead of him had a sign on the window.

He counted fourteen cars in a row, some with yellow printed signs on suction cups, some homemade paper and tape creations, but all bore a common message. The message was aimed at potential infiltrators and they ranged from informative to downright offensive. "NO RADIO," "NO CAR PHONE," or "COBRA IN BACK," they proclaimed. This was intended to dissuade the youth of our country from engaging in their favorite metropolitan pastime — vandalism for profit.

As Rabbi Wein approached the fifteenth car, he noticed the natives had not been deterred. The "NO RADIO" sign was still hanging from the smashed window and on the dashboard where the stereo used to be was taped a second sign: "YOU LIED." At that point, Rabbi Wein decided that twenty-seven dollars for a couple hours of parking was a very reasonable charge.

He drove his car around the block to a parking lot a lot closer to where he was going. As the parking attendant took his keys and gave him a ticket, a sleek new Lexus pulled in — "One of those cars" (Infiniti-Maseratti-Jaguar-etc.) is the way the Rabbi put it.

"Get that thing out of here!" barked the attendant.

The man hopped out of his car and began to shout. "You don't understand," he said. "I have an appointment with a client in five minutes. I must park now."

"Can't you read the sign?" he said with the air that comes from one who knows he has already won the argument. The sign read: 'No Mercedes, Jaguars, Ferraris, Alfa Romeo, Lexus . . .' The list went on to name many cars that Rabbi Wein never even heard of.

The driver began to plead: "I'll pay you a hundred dollars . . . two hundred dollars . . . you must take my car; I'm going to be late and they'll cancel the deal."

"Hey man," said the attendant, "Insurance companies don't like to pay $8,000 for a bumper scratch, so you get that thing out of here or I'll have it towed." And he walked away.

The owner of the car noticed that Rabbi Wein was watching the interchange and he appealed to his witness. "Did you see what just happened?" he asked.

The Rabbi nodded.

"What do you think I should do about this?"

Rabbi Wein pointed to his "rabbinical" Plymouth and offered a very interesting solution: "Want to trade cars?"

The man was in no mood for the Rabbi's proposal and then did what any sensible luxury car owner would do in a similar predicament: he sat down on the pavement and wept.

> There are a hundred lessons to be taken from this vignette. However, Rabbi Wein likes to use this story to illustrate the idea that we live in a world of unfolding vignettes. "They are all around us, but first we must notice them," Rabbi Wein is also fond of saying. "One has to notice the small things in life because it is the detail that reveals the great moments."

Stretch Limo

A very wealthy Jew phoned Rabbi Wein with a serious request. Several of his friends were interested in becoming more observant and wanted the Rabbi to teach them about the Purim holiday.

Rabbi Wein consented to help them, but because of their schedules they could meet only at night in the city. The Rabbi agreed to give the class at that time but asked that transportation be provided. After dark, he has a tendency to fall asleep at the wheel.

On the appointed evening, a chauffeur-driven, stretch limousine pulled up in front of his house. A bit overwhelmed by the size and luxury of the vehicle, the Rabbi got in. The interior was almost as big as his living room. There was a wet bar, a television set, a phone, and a foot massager built into the transaxle. A small refrigerator opened from the back of the front seats and was stocked with seltzer. "I could get used to this," he thought.

As they sped down the Palisades, Rabbi Wein was enjoying himself. He tinkered with some of the gadgets and poured a cup of seltzer. When he recalled that night he said, "If Fax machines had been invented at that time, that limo would have had two of them and I would have been playing with both." Before he knew it, they had reached the George Washington Bridge and the driver paid the toll.

The car was about to loop onto the bridge when Rabbi Wein spotted a Chassidic man standing off to the side of the road trying to hitch. He was hand signaling like an Israeli, with his index finger, and not like an American, with a thumb. As the car moved closer to where he was standing, the Rabbi recognized him as an Israeli *meshulach* (fundrasier) who earlier that day had come to his house in Monsey to solicit funds for his charity.

"Please pull over; I want to give that man a ride," he instructed the chauffeur.

The driver obliged. The *meshulach* hesitated at the sight of the limousine, but when he saw the Rabbi motion to him from the window, he boarded. His eyes ran quickly over the luxurious equipment. He inspected the bar, the phone, and the television set, and then looked at Rabbi Wein for an explanation, who just sat there as if this was an ordinary Sunday evening excursion.

"Where are you headed?" asked the Rabbi. The *meshulach* told him to drop him off at the nearest subway station. He didn't want to be a bother. "Besides I'm going all the way down the west side of Manhattan," he said.

"Just give the driver the address and we'll let you off at your door," Rabbi Wein suggested. And so they traveled in silence down the West Side Highway. The silence disturbed the hitchhiker, though. He turned to Rabbi Wein and asked. "This car, you rented it for the night, maybe?"

"No."

"It belongs to the synagogue on a lease?"

Rabbi Wein gave him a more laconic, "No."

Finally, as they were exiting the highway onto the side streets, "It's a *sheroot* possibly? (In Israel, *sheroot* is the name for a shared taxi that take people to the airports.) You're going to pick up more people?"

"No, it's not." And with that the Rabbi expertly poured a glass of seltzer into a paper cup and offered it to the befuddled mendicant. The poor man made a blessing and sipped slowly. His hands ran over the expensive velour which covered the seats.

Savoring the feel, the *meshulach* asked. "Is this how all American rabbis travel?" Rabbi Wein smiled and stared straight ahead. The Chassidic man nodded and settled back into his comfortable seat for the remainder of the trip.

They reached his destination. Before getting out, the *meshulach* shook the Rabbi's hand and gave him a hearty "*Yasher koach* (thank you)." He smiled knowingly at the Rabbi and said, "Now I finally understand why American rabbis do not move to *Eretz Yisroel*."

Asleep at the Wheel

When there are no limos to pick him up, Rabbi Wein has one of his boys at the yeshiva drive him. As a last resort he will drive into the city alone. One evening he was going to Brooklyn and was very apprehensive about driving at night — he has a tendency, when tired, to get very drowsy behind the wheel.

However, as he got to the entrance of the George Washington Bridge, he saw a Chassidic man standing at the side of the road looking for a ride. Rabbi Wein pulled over and picked him up. "Great," he thought, "someone who will talk to me and keep me awake."

But after the man got in, he did not say one word. He just folded his arms and snapped his eyelids shut. "Just what I needed," grumbled Rabbi Wein to himself, "another sleeper."

Soon the Rabbi found himself growing very, very tired. He opened his window to let the cold air in. He turned on the radio to some classical music and drove on hoping he could stay awake. After a few minutes of music, the Chassidic man opened his eyes, turned to him and asked, "Isn't this Mahler's Ninth?"

A bit stunned, Rabbi Wein answered that yes, indeed, it sounded like Mahler's music. "Then," the Rabbi reported, "we began to discuss everything from classical music to *halachah* and *kabbalah* (mysticism). It was one of the most fascinating and animated conversations I ever had in my life, and the trip to Brooklyn that normally takes forever was over in two minutes."

As Rabbi Wein prepared to drop him off, his riding companion turned to him and asked, "Where are you from?"

"I'm from Monsey," Rabbi Wein answered.

"Where in Monsey?"

"Up the hill."

"Up the hill, where?" the Chassid persisted. "Where do you *daven* (pray)?"

"I *daven* at Bais Torah."

"Oh, isn't that Rabbi Wein's synagogue?"

"Yes," answered Rabbi Wein. "Rabbi Wein is the Rav of the synagogue."

"Well, if he has *baalei batim* (congregants) like you," the Chassid continued, "he must have a very difficult time coming up with something to say."

Rabbi Wein smiled, "You don't know how difficult."

On the Road Again

Many times, when he is traveling, Rabbi Wein will be spotted by a complete stranger, someone who probably heard him speak from the back of a dining hall and was too distant to recall him exactly. These people all approach the Rabbi warily and circle around trying not to stare. Rabbi Wein recognizes this as the reconnoitering phase — getting the lay of his facial land, so to speak. When they are sure of his I.D. they move into the greeting phase, certain of their quarry.

On a flight from Los Angeles, one such passenger was moving in for the greeting.

"Hi there, I'm Phil Cohen from Teaneck. I think I know you; you're Rabbi Wein, aren't you?"

"Yes, I am," Rabbi Wein said.

"Your father was the head of O.U., wasn't he?"

Flattered beyond words, Rabbi Wein lapsed into silence. "So much for the rewards of fame," he remarks.

The Jewish History Tapes

In 1985, Rabbi Wein began his now famous Jewish History tape series. These audiotapes explain Jewish history from an Orthodox point of view and have been the most widely traveled Wein emissary. Rabbi Wein adds, "Sony and Fuji think they're in the business of consumer electronics — but their tapes' true purpose is to disseminate God's message around the globe."

It was just after midnight when the Rabbi's phone rang. Any call that late is usually either an emergency or bad timing, but this time it was neither. The caller was a man from Nairobi, Kenya who had gotten hold of Rabbi Wein's Jewish History tape series. "I have a question about Agrippa and the rise of Christianity," he said.

After Rabbi Wein clarified a few details for him, this man told the Rabbi about his community. "We have a small Jewish community here but it is quickly dying out. There is no Jewish school for the children to attend and without any education one can not expect they will carry on any sort of Jewish tradition.

"I myself have little Jewish education," the man continued. "I cannot even read Hebrew. But the children, Rabbi, someone had to do something for the children. So I took it upon myself to teach them whatever I knew. I organized a learning group for the boys and girls in my town and taught them about Passover, about the Sabbath; but, as I said, my knowledge is very limited and I quickly ran out of material.

"Then I discovered your tapes and I cannot begin to describe the impact of your lectures. I listen to one tape each week and prepare the class from it. The children are fascinated by the stories of the Maccabees and the Temple. We have discussions that last past class time and one can see the Jewish identity of these children surfacing."

After exchanging "thank you"s, the caller did mention that he had one complaint. "It took me forever to get hold of your telephone number. Why aren't you listed in the phone book under "Rabbi?"

> No one knows precisely why the Rabbi prefers to be listed as just plain Berel. Is it his anivus (humility), his Lithuanian disdain for notoriety or is it simply that when he was asked to supply his correct name and title to the telephone company, he was newly arrived in Monsey and not working as a Rabbi? No one knows. But everyone who needs to talk with him gets through nonetheless.

Reserved

Some of Rabbi Wein's most cherished memories come from the time he spent with Rabbi Yosef Kahaneman, the Ponevezher Rav. The Rav would come to Miami to raise funds for his yeshiva and Rabbi Wein had the privilege of being his driver during his short stays. Each year the Rav would insist on visiting the famous Miami Aquarium because, "He loved to see the fish. He marveled at God's creations."

The Ponevezher Rav saw life differently from most people. During the Second World War, Palestine, still under the British mandate, was threatened by Hitler's army in the area, General Erwin Rommel's famed Afrika Korps. The Germans were positioned at Alexandria, Egypt, a ten-day march from Tel Aviv and the Jewish population was in a near panic. The Jewish Agency began destroying many of its files and hiding others. The Torah leaders proclaimed community fasting, and *tachrichim* (burial shrouds) were prepared by the thousands as the small community braced itself for the worst.

While Rommel's troops awaited orders to begin the march to the Holy Land, Rav Kahaneman arrived in Israel, in the port city of Yaffo. Committed to pick up where he had left off in Ponevezhe, he made plans to begin building a yeshiva in his new home of Bnei Brak. "Rebbe," they said to him, "you are being foolish. The Nazis could be here in ten days. Then what will be with your yeshiva?"

The Rav dismissed the argument. "Even if they do come," he said, "it is worth it to have the yeshiva even for ten days."

The Rav sensed the urgency of the situation but recognized that one can not plan too far in advance. And, indeed, the Ponevezher Yeshiva is still open to this day.

Rav Kahaneman carried his philosophy with him on fundraising tours as well. Once he had an appointment in downtown Miami with a very wealthy businessman. Rabbi Wein had set up the meeting himself with quite a bit of effort. The man had canceled several times previously and Rabbi Wein was determined not to allow this chance to slip away also. They drove to the man's office with what they thought was plenty of time, but heavy traffic and poor directions changed all that. They had a three o'clock appointment and pulled into the building's parking lot at two minutes to the hour.

Unfortunately, the parking lot was full except for one spot just in front of the main entrance. "Pull in over there," Rav Kahaneman said. It seemed too good to be true, and indeed it was. As they got closer they saw the sign in front of the spot: RESERVED FOR THE PRESIDENT.

"I guess we can't park there," Rabbi Wein said scanning the area for alternatives.

"Don't worry," the Rav said, "just pull in."

"But, Rebbe, it says . . . "

"Trust me. Park there."

Rabbi Wein pulled in and the two hurried out of the car into the air-conditioned lobby. They took the elevator up eight flights. As soon as the doors opened to the office, Rabbi Wein rushed over to the secretary, gave his name and stated his business. They were immediately shown into a suite of offices which took up half the floor. At the far end, by an enormous picture window overlooking Miami Beach, sat a small, balding man behind his glass and ivory desk. He stood up for the two rabbis. "Welcome, Rabbi, welcome."

Rabbi Wein introduced Rav Kahaneman, who had been forewarned that their meeting could not last longer than ten minutes. The Rav began his sales pitch for the yeshiva.

"No one was a better fundraiser than the Ponevezher Rav," Rabbi Wein recalls. "He could walk out with a check that others wouldn't dare dream of."

Rabbi Wein simply sat back and watched the master at work. Rav Kahaneman's stories captivated his one-man audience. With only two minutes left, as the Rav was shifting into his climax, a sharply dressed man barged into the room. His face was almost as red as his tie.

"These men have taken your parking spot, sir."

Rabbi Wein felt like sinking into the couch he had been sitting on. The Ponevezher Rav had insisted they use that parking spot; he said to trust him and that is exactly what Rabbi Wein did. He looked down at floor as the Rav smiled and turned back to the president.

"Let me explain," the Rav said. "We stopped and called fifteen minutes before we came and the secretary told us you were in. When we arrived there was no car in that spot so we knew you didn't need it. We needed a place for our car so we put it there."

The assistant was nonplused. "That sign says, 'RESERVED.' "

"Despite what the sign may say," the Rav countered, "It was our spot for the taking. In this world, God gives us many things but he never gives them for us to keep. A house is bought and sold. Money is transferred from place to place, from person to person. What we have is ours only for the time that it is in our hands. For that period God gives it to us to see what we can do with it. Eventually a man dies and his children get the money — then it is their turn to play with it. 'Reserved' does not exist. If you are not using something properly, then God may just give it to someone else who will use it in the correct fashion."

Though the assistant was not impressed with the Rav's explanation, the senior executive was grinning broadly, well aware that the Rav was not just talking about parking cars. The Rav's ten minutes were up and by the time he got up to go he had received a very large donation.

In return, the president received from the Rav a Kahaneman trademark, a prolonged and noisy kiss. The Rav loved Jews and loved to express his joy by kissing them on their cheeks. When he saw this, the assistant couldn't believe his eyes. He threw up his hands and walked out of the office, away from the spectacle of this effusive, elderly Rabbi kissing the boss after taking his "reserved" parking space.

Chapter 1: On the Road Again ☐ *43*

The assistant placed great importance in external "signs." Americans, in general, also hold by credentials. If the paper on the wall says this medical school or that law school we are comforted. One of the critics who reviewed Rabbi Wein's book "Triumph of Survival" criticized it because Rabbi Wein didn't have a Ph.D. in Jewish history. He may have been a lawyer, a very learned Rabbi, a lecturer in Jewish history, an international scholar invited to represent the Orthodox Jewish point of view at historical seminars around the world, but for this critic, Rabbi Wein's version of history is irrelevant because he didn't have appropriate credentials as a historian.

In modern times, when all the old assumptions are being questioned, our over-dependence on certificates of expertise is dangerous. Rav Kahaneman seemed to say the same thing — that if you were given something and didn't use it, it did not matter who you were. Don't go by signs; go by people.

L'Shaim Shamayim

Rabbi Wein: "God wants us to perfect our talents — our task is to realize that we have God-given talents and we have to make sure we use these gifts to glorify his name — l'shaim shamayim (literally, for the sake of heaven)."

"Shaarei Chesed is one of the oldest neighborhoods in Jerusalem. It was founded about ninety years ago and it has 137 homes. Why that number? Because the planner had a sheet of paper that could be divided into 137 lots. If he had a bigger paper there would have been more houses. That tells you a lot about how they used to live in Jerusalem around the turn of the century."

Rabbi Wein continues: "In the middle of Rehov Hakalir sits the Gr'a Synagogue and it's what is affectionately called a '*minyan* factory.' One can find a *minyan* of ten or more men almost any time. However, the last *minyan* starts at 9:30 at night. To that *minyan* comes one of the great rabbis in the Jewish world, Rabbi Shlomo Zalman Auerbach. He's a fixture in Shaarei Chesed; he's been living there for eighty years and has been active in the community all that time. His son is Dean in the yeshiva that is housed in the second floor above the synagogue.

"Among the regulars to that *minyan* is Reb Yissachar, a street cleaner for the city of Jerusalem. One often sees him with his broom and mobile garbage can sweeping the streets of Rechaviah and Shaarei Chesed. After evening prayers, Reb Yissachar teaches the older men a portion of *halachah* from the *Mishnah Brurah*.

"One night, an American tourist and I decided to attend the 9:30 *minyan*. We were about to begin when we heard Rav Auerbach delay the prayers: "Reb Yissachar, the street cleaner, is not here," he announced. "We have to wait for him."

"The American tourist was a little perturbed and asked Rav Auerbach, 'We're three minutes late already. Why do we have to wait for a street cleaner?'

" 'You don't understand,' came the reply. 'He may be just a street cleaner but he cleans the streets *l'shaim shamayim,* for the sake of heaven.' Then he thought about it for a minute. 'I wish,' he said, 'that I had the *l'shaim shamayim* in my job that he has in his job.' "

"And this," Rabbi Wein interjects, "came from a man who sits all day in front of sacred literature, answering peoples' questions, and constantly working to perfect his Torah knowledge."

The Rabbi then deftly picks up the story's concluding thread. "As if on cue Reb Yissachar flew through the doors, the prayers commenced and the tourist was mollified."

This is one of the many vignettes that contribute to the magical ambiance of the city of Jerusalem. A street cleaner, a world famous Rav, and an aggressive tourist demanding prayers start on time. But in this city, let it be understood, the streets are cleaned *l'shaim shamayim.*

The Chanukah Clock

One Chanukah, Rabbi Wein was the keynote speaker of an Orthodox convention of scholars in Minneapolis, Minnesota. The organizers booked him into the Marriot Hotel, a newly built edifice right in the center of town. His room was on the twenty-fourth floor and it looked out over a large park surrounded by office buildings. In the middle of the lot stood a huge Norway spruce that served as the city's Christmas tree. Christmas was just around the corner and the tree was splendidly decorated, thousands of lights illuminating its towering branches.

Rabbi Wein scanned the windows of the office buildings that circled the park and nary a *menorah* was to be seen. It depressed him; he pulled the curtains shut. In ten minutes he was to make the keynote address in the convention and dispiritedly he sat down to polish his speech. The room opened onto an alcove that was partially hidden by two glass French doors. Through them the Rabbi saw another Christmas tree; it too was decorated with tiny little Christmas lights.

The Christmas trees were inescapable, so Rabbi Wein opened one of the closets and found an extra blanket folded on the shelf. He took it down, went to the alcove, covered the tree with the blanket, and unplugged the lights on the tree. Now with only five minutes left he took the speech off the desk and left his room, taking the elevator to the Banquet Room. As he got to the dais he discovered that he forgot his glasses back in his room, so he quickly got back on the elevator and returned to his room. On the door of the room, he noticed a Christmas wreath that wasn't there when he left a few minutes before. He walked in to find the maid tidying up, putting a chocolate mint on his pillow, and folding his towels. To her amazement, when she opened the French doors she saw that the Christmas tree was covered.

"Now, who could have done that?" she asked.

Rabbi Wein shook his head in feigned disbelief. She stripped the blanket off the tree, folded it, and plugged the light cord back into the socket.

Now the lights were blinking very brightly into the room, and the maid, working cheerily, went back to her chores. After finding his glasses, Rabbi Wein paused before he went down to the main ballroom. He sadly reflected that there was nothing there to remind him of Chanukah.

"It's all so depressing," he thought. The blinking lights guarded by the hovering, watchful maid; the city scene dominated by the pagan Norway spruce; the Christmas wreaths that hung across the door to his room: "It's all so overwhelmingly Christmassy. Where was Channukah?"

Just before he left, he noticed on top of the fireplace sat an "Atmosphere Clock." The clock is a timepiece that does not run on batteries, electricity, or winding. The mechanism receives its energy from subtle temperature changes and almost miraculously does not need any alternate source of energy. Its energies are hidden.

Rabbi Wein examined it closely. "A clock that runs on no visible fuel. What else runs on no fuel?" he asked himself. Immediately this clock became in his mind the miraculous Chanukah light that needed only one days' supply of oil to burn for eight days. It was the most beautiful *menorah* substitute he had ever seen. Even in the antiseptic Marriott, in a lonely and strange city, one can find God, he thought.

Like a redeemed Scrooge he called out a hearty good night to the maid and flew down the hall just in time to deliver a joyous welcome to the Chanukah conventioneers.

Saddam and Me

Rabbi Wein was standing in the airport terminal in front of a ticket attendant who was staring into her computer screen.

"I'm sorry sir, but I don't see your name." After she checked with her supervisor, Rabbi Wein was forced to accept the conclusion that he was stranded at the airport without a ticket. Invited out of town so often to speak at yeshiva banquets, community functions, and synagogues, as a Scholar in Residence, he knew it was bound to happen. He was expected at a speaking engagement, but the ticket never came. It didn't arrive in the mail and it wasn't waiting for him at the terminal.

The Rabbi reached for his wallet, pulled out an American Express card (he has been a card member since 1974, though he's never been asked to appear in an advertisement) and waited to hear the price. When one wants to buy an airline ticket, the most inexpensive way is to pay at least seven days in advance, fly on a weekday and stay over a Saturday night. On the other hand, the most expensive way is to get to the airport and buy a ticket ten minutes before the flight.

"Six hundred forty-two dollars," the lady said cheerfully, lifting her face from the computer screen.

"My first thought as she took the credit card," Rabbi Wein told us, "was that for a hundred dollars less I could have flown to Tel Aviv."

But for all that money, they treat you nicely on the plane. Rabbi Wein was entitled to a free copy of the *Wall Street Journal,* which he thumbed through with disinterest. His thoughts were elsewhere. It was January 15, 1991, and that night the United States would declare war on Saddam Hussein and Iraq. Several of his students had chosen that day to fly to Israel and Rabbi Wein thought of them as his plane took off for Detroit.

After a half hour in the air, a woman sitting a couple of seats over, who had been pecking away at her laptop computer the whole time, glanced up and noticed Rabbi Wein's *Wall Street Journal.*

"Do you mind if I have a look at your paper?" she asked. "I'd like to take a look at my portfolio."

Rabbi Wein handed it to her. In a few minutes her disappointed groans became audible. All the stocks had fallen in anticipation of the war, and with the recession underway the overall financial outlook was bleak.

After ten minutes of disheartening reading, the woman gave the paper back to Rabbi Wein and, taking note of his rabbinical garb, said in exasperation, "You know that this is all your fault."

"Madam," Rabbi Wein said, "you are correct but you have expressed yourself inelegantly. It is not my *fault*; it is because of me."

Hakol bishvil Yisroel, Rabbi Wein explains to his students. "Everything happens for the sake of the Jews. Even the lady of the airplane senses that. We did not ask for the Persian Gulf War, but as soon as the United States threatened Iraq, Saddam Hussein responded with his own threats against Israel. The Jews always get caught in the middle because that is where the good Lord wants us to be.

"The Soviet Union was brought to its knees by less than fifty Jews; people like refuseniks Scharansky, Nudel, Grilius, and Mendelevich; Jews who risked everything to be more Jewish, to move to Israel. Today any Jew can move to Israel — it's the only way out of the country. If you want to leave the Soviet Union you have to say you are Jewish. Isn't that ironic?

"My most recent trip to Israel came at the end of the war. I was there just in time for the last Scud attack, sitting in the sealed room of the hotel with nine other guests and the assistant manager, who was helping everyone put on the masks. Then we just sat down on the floor listening to Nachman Shai, an Israeli general, on the radio. He was counting down the minutes that it takes the Scud to fly from Iraq. 'Seven minutes,' he would announce, 'six minutes,' and in between they would play soft, soothing music. During the final minute we waited anxiously until General Shai came on and told us in that delicious Israeli irony: 'If you did not hear an explosion by this time, the missile did not land near you.' We took off our masks and left the room. I headed straight for the front door and stepped outside into the cold Jerusalem night to reflect upon my experience.

"I have been to Israel many times, been a Rav for over twenty-five years, and an orthodox Jew all my life. Yet never have I felt more Jewish. Saddam was not only attacking Israel; he meant me too. I'm an American citizen. I'm a pretty nice guy. But he wants me dead along with everyone else because I am a Jew."

> Thirty-nine Scuds were fired at Eretz Yisroel. Seventeen arrived, fourteen landed in populated areas, destroying over two thousand apartments and homes in the greater Tel Aviv area — the most densely populated part of the country — yet only two people were killed as a direct result of the Scuds.
>
> In 1981, Israel destroyed a nuclear facility in Iraq. The first country to speak against Israel in the General Assembly of the United Nations was Kuwait. Between the destruction of the regional infrastructure and the air pollution caused by sabotage of the oil wells, Kuwait will never be the same.
>
> God measures out his justice exceedingly fine — to a hairsbreadth.

The Big Joke

As a frequent flier, Rabbi Wein invariably runs into all sorts of people. Once, while moving to his seat on a flight to Chicago he heard gales of laughter emanating from the first class cabin. Rabbi Wein had to pass first class on the way to his seat and he saw a man with an anvil-shaped jaw and the face of a twelve-year-old reclining, legs outstretched, surrounded by stewardesses, passengers, and the co-pilot.

"He was making all sorts of cracks, kidding around about the airline's safety record, questioning the pilot's competence, insulting the investment bankers across the aisle, and everyone was enjoying it thoroughly."

The Rabbi reached his seat, which happened to be close to the festivities, and for the ten minutes that the Rabbi watched, the man did not utter one serious sentence. He had absolutely nothing positive to say, nothing meaningful to contribute.

Rabbi Wein is a big believer in having a sense of humor, but this fellow was overdoing it. "I love humor as much as the next guy," Rabbi Wein explains, "but this man was too much. They told me he was the substitute host for a popular talk show. The man's whole life is comedy and he is so saturated with provoking laughter that he probably never sees anything in a serious light. Everything that happens to him is screened for humor: what joke can he filter from this experience? All he cares about is the next punchline.

"That," Rabbi Wein informs his students, "is where joking ends and the destructive nature of *leitzonis* (mockery) begins. When all a person wants to do is make wisecracks and turn every situation into a monologue he is in trouble. Life in America may be very funny but it is certainly not a joke."

The Rabbi and the Priest

The major hospital servicing the Monsey area is the Good Samaritan Hospital. One Saturday night Rabbi Wein was visiting a member of the congregation who was ill. The patient was in a room on the top floor, and after the visit the Rabbi went to take the elevator down.

Now, the hospital has two sets of elevators, each on opposite sides of one hall. As Rabbi Wein approached one elevator, standing at the opposite elevator, dressed in his full regalia, was a Roman Catholic priest who had just been visiting one of his own parishioners. There were a number of people waiting in the middle, between the two clergymen. The priest had just pushed the button for the elevator on his side of the hall as the Rabbi proceeded to push the elevator button on his side. Seeing Rabbi Wein still dressed in his Shabbos attire, the priest looked over at him and said, "Good evening, Rabbi." Rabbi Wein turned and politely replied, "Good evening, Father." And then they all stood there waiting for the elevator to come.

The people in the middle looked paralyzed, believing that the theological dispute of the centuries was about to be settled right before their eyes — which spiritual leader could command the first elevator. Rabbi Wein continues:

"All rumors to the contrary notwithstanding, God is on the side of Rabbis and the elevator on my side came first. The door slid open, I smiled, and magnanimously waved everyone in, including the priest, and we all started to go down in the elevator together. Then the priest looking over at me with a sly twinkle in his eye, remarked, 'Rabbi, what would you have said if my elevator had come first?'

"Father," I replied, "one cannot prove anything from a descending elevator."

> The Rabbi uses this story to comment on our world. "Whether we like it or not, our world — I think — is a descending elevator. Therefore, it's hard to prove anything from our society — its standards, values, and distorted sense of normalcy." Lest you think the Rabbi feels pessimistic about the Jewish world also being in descent, he is quick to respond: "No, I certainly feel we're not descending. Society is descending. What society calls 'normal,' and what society accepts, and what society attributes value to — we should not be so quick to accept; these values simply don't stand up; they are subject to instant revision, almost at a whim. So when I say

descending, I mean society is descending, but we don't have to descend with it.

I went to public school as a boy until the eighth grade and when I went to school in the morning the boys and the girls had separate entrances. That was public school at a time when we were being taught a different set of values. Today, in public schools, sixth graders have severe drug problems, and on Open School Night it's hard to find five parents who feel motivated to talk to teachers. It's so discouraging. So we're talking about a different society — different values and different problems. Therefore, we have to hang on hard to what we know is correct. Just because everyone else is crazy doesn't mean I have to act crazy too."

2
Food for Thought

---

*"Life is like chewing gum —
a little flavor
and the rest is chew, chew, chew . . ."*

Rabbi Mendel Kaplan

Food For Thought

hen he first took over the directorship of the O.U., Rabbi Wein felt the best way to find out what was going on in the organization was to make a surprise visit to the field. "Let's see the troops function under real life pressure with no advance warning," was the way he put it. He checked his calendar and

selected a wedding at a catering hall located along the Long Island Sound in the Bronx.

Arriving early, the Rabbi took off his coat and began to take in the scene. Still too new to the New York area to be recognized, he was free to observe the proceedings. Visiting the kitchen, he saw that the caterer was setting up his food trays. He asked for the *mashgiach* (kosher food supervisor) and was told that he was not there "right now."

Rabbi Wein casually mixed among the guests. The wine and the liquor bottles all had appropriate *hechshairim* (kosher certification); the cake looked kosher enough, but when he asked someone who baked it, he was given a fishy stare and asked: "Are you the *mashgiach*?"

"No," Rabbi Wein answered. "I'm looking for him myself."

"Go to the hall where the *kallah* (bride) sits," came the reply.

In the main reception area, the smorgasbord table was particularly sumptuous; the caterer had spared no expense in the preparation. The eating had commenced; slices of roast beef and corned beef and pastrami were flying through the air and the baby lamb chops and sweetbreads were disappearing at the speed of light. They even had a sushi section which was seeing a lot of action, too. But when the Japanese sushi slicer was asked the *mashgiach's* whereabouts, he looked in the direction of the bandstand and gravely confessed he didn't know. "Maybe that's him sitting next to the drummer," he indicated with his cleaver. Rabbi Wein continued to search.

Rabbi Wein returned to the kitchen and asked pointedly, "I need to see the *mashgiach* right now." The cooks directed him to the outside. "He likes to take a smoke," they said.

There he spotted a lone man in shirtsleeves smoking a cigarette and sitting on a balustrade. He was gazing at the water, enjoying the breezes of the Sound. Rabbi Wein sauntered over to him and started a conversation.

"Are you with the groom or the bride?" Rabbi Wein asked.

"Neither. I'm working here today; I'm the *mashgiach*."

Rabbi Wein didn't know the man and was sure the man didn't know him. "There are a lot of people in there."

The *mashgiach* supplied an estimate, "Six or seven hundred."

"Look," said Rabbi Wein, "I don't mean to tell you your business but shouldn't you be inside checking on the food and the service?"

"Nah," came the reply, "everything is alright."

"How do you know?"

The *mashgiach* flipped his cigarette into the water below him. "How do I know? What could go wrong? It's under O.U. supervision, isn't it?"

> In one version of this story, Rabbi Wein meets up with his mashgiach at the smorgasboard dipping carrot sticks into the salad dressing. Whichever the case, afterwards O.U. supervision tightened up considerably. In monthly meetings with his kashruth supervisors, he urged them to stay vigilant. "You never know when I'm going to show up, so stay on your toes. If I am not here for the O.U., I might just show up as the m'sader kiddushin (Officiating Rabbi).

Chocolate Bar

One of Rabbi Wein's chief accomplishments as president of the O.U. was that he was able to persuade a large American food company to accept rabbinical supervision on their consumer and industrial products. The company remains kosher until today. However, the average consumer wouldn't know it because they don't put it on their label. Until recently, it was the largest company in the world that had no advertising budget. They didn't believe in it.

So, when it came to compensating the O.U. for their work, the company had a problem. Most companies the O.U. deals with have no Division of Kosher Supervision from which to draw funds. If you want to get paid you have to feed something into the computer that it understands. Business expenses such as labor, materials, insurance, etc., do not describe the services provided by a kashruth supervisor.

"We don't advertise and there's no category that fits your service, so how am I going to pay you?" asked the comptroller.

And he was dead serious. As Rabbi Wein tells it, "This man was the chief financial officer of a billion dollar company that's making 800 million jelly beans an hour and he can't find a way to pay us."

I thought about it for a moment and told him to pay us out of the department for legal services. Since kosher certification is a consideration which is subjected to numerous regulations, it seemed most appropriate. He took that suggestion to the head of their legal department, who loved the idea. We got paid from the Division of Legal Services, Sub-Department of Product Liability (which, if you think about it, is not far from the truth).

Rabbi Wein then met with the President of the company in his office. He describes the encounter:

"The room defied description. His desk alone could float the yeshiva for a month. I asked him straight out, 'How come you guys don't have an advertising budget?' He gave three reasons:

" 'Number one,' he said, 'we have made money every year for a hundred forty years, so we are doing well without it. Number two, it's an additional headache. To establish an advertising department, we would have to deal with advertising agencies, wrestle with problems of image and so forth. We are a low profile company. This is a company town and the people are very loyal. If you work for us, you work forever. In the advertising game personnel turnover is a fact of life and it's not our style to fire anyone.

" 'However, Rabbi, these are not the main reasons,' he added. 'The main reason we don't advertise is because the advertising in this country is not honest.'

"I couldn't believe my ears," says Rabbi Wein. "This is a non-Jewish businessman telling me this, and he's one hundred percent right. He knows the *halachah*! Don't mislead your neighbor (*ganaivas da'as*). According to Jewish law, it is very hard to approve of the way products are advertised in this country. There's too much seductive advertising which promises one thing and delivers something quite different. After we finished our business, I thanked him for his time and left."

As he drove home from Pennsylvania, Rabbi Wein remembers feeling exhilarated by the encounter with the President of the company. That week he wrote a memo to the staff of the O.U. "If everybody is doing the wrong thing, nothing is wrong. In other words, if everyone cheats in business, the complaint against each one is lessened because: 'That's business.' But if there's someone who is not doing it, then all the rest have no answer. God has one company that obligates (*mechayev*) all the other companies.

> "There is always one who is *mechayav* others. Our rabbis say that Joseph, Yaakov's son, is *mechayev* those who are handsome. It is a terrible burden to be handsome; it's even worse for a woman to be beautiful. The temptations can be overwhelming, but Joseph held himself back. He successfully restrained himself and therefore obligated (was *mechayev*) all the handsome men of this world to act normally.
>
> "Hillel is *mechayav* poor people. A poor person would claim he has no time to go the yeshiva and learn Torah because he had to scratch out a living. So Hillel, who was at least as poor as any man, found a way to learn nevertheless. By sacrificing so much for learning Torah he was *mechayev* all other people.
>
> "Rebbi, Rabbi Judah the Prince, is *mechayev* the wealthy people. People claim they are so busy with business and investments that they haven't got time to learn. Rebbi was one of the wealthiest people in the world. He also found time to compile the Mishnah and be a great Talmudic teacher. Thus he

obligates rich people. No one can ever plead that circumstances were too overwhelming for him to learn.

"When it comes to advertising, this company obligates the business world. They take away the excuses of all the other companies because someone will come and say. 'But I have to advertise to stay in business.' And this is what advertising is: '$99 TO FLORIDA' in tremendous letters while on the bottom it says that you have to go on a Tuesday and come back Thursday and rent a car and bring your mother-in-law and don't breathe the air. That's advertising. So God made one company that doesn't advertise. A company that says, it pays **not** to advertise. A company that wants to stay truthful."

Und Vos Zugt Gott?

Rabbi Alexander Rosenberg founded the Kashruth Division of the Union of Orthodox Union Jewish Congregations of America, commonly known as the O.U., and served as its chief administrator for over thirty years. He was a highly intelligent man with searing blue eyes that could penetrate to the core of a person. For a number of months Rabbi Wein served in the same office with this aristocratic man.

He recalls: "When you're the head of O.U., people gravitate toward you with all sorts of proposals. It's the nature of the business. I remember how Rabbi Rosenberg would just sit there and silently listen to the latest proposals which the salesmen claimed would enhance Rabbi Rosenberg and the stature of the O.U., in addition to being a great boon to civilization."

"Rabbi Rosenberg would patiently wait for the salesman to make his spiel and then he would just peer at him with those hooded blue eyes. Then he would pounce, falcon-like, and ask just one question that was comprised of but four words — Und vos zugt Gott?' (And what does God say?) Does it check out? Would you tell the IRS such a story? 'Und vos zugt Gott?' "

Rabbi Wein says he's used this story so many times that his students one year bought him a plaque for his office that says just that — "Und vos zugt Gott?"

Well, it happened that when the Arab oil embargo hit the United States in 1973, Rabbi Wein received a phone call from the production manager of a large pharmaceutical company warning him that a production crisis loomed if he didn't receive a sizable shipment of glycerin. (The O.U. had been working with the company in their production of vitamin tablets and liquids and various other kosher nutritional supplements and they were the first to become a user of O.U. certified synthetic chemicals in producing pharmaceuticals. Most children's vitamins are made in 75% glycerin solution. In addition, there are two ways to make glycerin: out of animal fat, and the kosher way, chemically, from crude oil.)

"Rabbi Wein," the manager began, "we've got a problem. I can't get any delivery of the glycerin because the suppliers can't obtain any crude oil to process. I've got a million labels with 'O.U.' printed on them and there's no way I can take the certification off the label."

Rabbi Wein began to detect a note of not so quiet desperation in his voice. The man continued.

"Rabbi, it might take me ten days to get a million new labels printed without the O.U. mark." Now came the ultimatum. "Unless you locate eight carloads of kosher synthetic glycerin for me, I'm going to have to fall back on the other kind of glycerin, and I don't plan to close down my production line for two weeks just to correct my labels."

To send out notices to all the synagogues and institutions that the vitamin was not to be used for two weeks would call the integrity of the O.U. into question. Rabbi Wein was also sensitive to the human relations aspects of the problem. He didn't want to jeopardize an excellent working relationship with the pharmaceutical companies that his predecessor, Rabbi Rosenberg, had taken years to establish. The pharmaceutical industry was a hard nut to crack and now that it had agreed to certification, yanking the Rabbinical approval for two weeks would have undermined public trust in the companies involved.

There was only one thing to do said Rabbi Wein, "We set out to find kosher glycerin; it was a quest for the holy fat."

This is the way Rabbi Wein described the hunt, "The production manager gave me a list of suppliers across the United States, which we narrowed down to two giant manufacturers. Only those two produced oil-based glycerin in sufficiently large quantities to have a surplus eight carloads lying around their rail yards.

"At first we called one of the companies but they were uncooperative. Any oil-derived products were closely watched and if they had any surplus they weren't letting on. That left me with the other company, which had a huge production facility located at the center of the company's operation."

He continued, "After trying to reach the production manager at the company for an hour and having my calls transferred all around, I finally got him on the line. But he told me pretty much the same story as the first company did — if they had any surplus, their regular customers would get it. I had to think fast, we were running out of time.

"I did have one connection on the executive board of that company who might be helpful. Rabbi Rosenberg once mentioned that this man was sympathetic to our needs, but it took me another hour to get through to this executive.

"I explained our plight to him. I made him understand that he was the supplier of last resort and I tried to make him see what the drug certification program meant to us and to Jewry in the United States. He listened carefully and when I was finished he didn't answer right away. My pulse quickened as I waited on the phone for his response.

" 'Call and tell them I'm going to release some of our production run to you,' he said. 'I think I can find eight carloads, but, Rabbi,

I want some assurances.'

" 'Yes,' I said relieved. 'We'll try to give you whatever you need.' I was sure he was going to talk price and buying commitments.

" 'I just want to make sure,' he continued, 'that Rabbi Rosenberg in heaven knows what I'm doing.' I did not comprehend. 'I know he's dead,' he continued, 'but I want you to make sure Rabbi Rosenberg hears about this.'

"Rabbi Rosenberg passed away a few years before. While he was training me for the job a few months before his retirement, he had impressed upon me the importance of our work. 'Kashruth is more than checking chickens,' he used to say, 'The job of the O.U. is to pay attention to God. *'Und vos zugt Gott?'* is the main concern. What would God say about this? is the question that must always be answered before making any decision.'

" *'Und vos zugt Gott?'* A question like that is bigger than knives and chickens, bigger even than the biggest food companies."

"What a *kiddush Hashem* (sanctification of God's Name) was expressed by that executive vice-president. He acknowledged that heaven existed; heaven was as real as the earth he was standing on and he knew there were holy people on earth as well.

"With a full heart I told him that his action would not go unnoticed in the highest spheres. I also reminded myself of the statement of our Sages that the life of a *tzaddik* (righteous man) can affect the living long after his death."

Bow-U

While it is generally permissible to benefit from non-kosher foods, there are exceptions. For example, mixtures of milk and meat are not only forbidden for eating but are also prohibited from all benefit. The most practical application of this *halachah* concerns pet food; one may not even feed his pet milk and meat compounds. Since many commercial animal foods contain this combination, it is important to use discretion when feeding one's pets.

A major company, in seeking to widen the marketability of its pet food line, got wind of this *halachah*. One of their executives contacted the O.U. about entering into a program to provide certification for their dog food.

Rabbi Wein admitted that it was a good idea, yet he turned the company down on the grounds that giving certification to dog food would would expose the O.U. to ridicule. The integrity of the organization and of the entire kashruth field had to be preserved.

"And so ended," Rabbi Wein explained, "the first and only attempt to receive a BOW-U certification."

Tzitzis

When Rabbi Wein was with the O.U., the chief *shochet* (ritual slaughterer) was a pious Jew, Rabbi Mendel Schwartz. (The name is fictitious but the man and the events are real.) He was already a *shochet* before the war in Warsaw. His family was killed by the Nazis but he survived the concentration camps and came to this country. Here he remarried and started over again as a *shochet* with the O.U.

Rabbi Wein says: "When he was in the death camps, he never ate *traife* (non-kosher food). He knew that if he survived, he wanted to continue as a *shochet*. In the Auschwitz camp, he subsisted on what he could find: bread, vegetables, anything permissible by Jewish dietary law. (*Shochtim* are not just butchers; they, themselves, need to be as stainless as the meat they prepare.)"

One day, Reb Mendel called Rabbi Wein to tell him that the following morning he intended to pick him up early because they had to go to the University of Connecticut where the School of Agriculture was working to develop a holding pen for the humane killing of sheep. Pens were originally devised to eliminate the problem of shackling animals, which inspires the perception of cruelty. Rabbi Wein explained, "This is an important issue here in the United States. The animal lovers are a very powerful lobby and can cause the kosher meat slaughtering industry no end of trouble. Therefore we try to develop more humane methods of *shechitah* (slaughtering)."

This time, though, Rabbi Wein's schedule was backed up with speaking commitments. "Listen, Rabbi Schwartz, this week I'm very busy and can't find the time to go with you."

"You've got to come," he replied. "If you don't show up tomorrow, they'll say we're not interested. We can't risk that," Reb Mendel persisted.

Rabbi Wein relented. "I knew he was right so we agreed to leave in the morning."

Upon arriving at the University they were directed to a barn that had six sheep penned up in the experimental enclosure. Rabbi Wein described what happened.

"We changed into our garments brought specially for the *shechitah*. We had rubber jump suits and helmets to cover our heads. There is a tremendous amount of blood during *shechitah*."

Looking around the barn, Rabbi Wein noticed there was no place to change in private. "As there were only men in that barn, we decided to change right there. The leader of this group was a twenty-five year old man in a Ph.D. program at the University. We were talking with him and found out the sheep pen was his dissertation project. When I asked him how he got interested in a *shechitah* project, he admitted, 'It's just some work that needed to be done, but maybe it's also because of my background. I'm Jewish, you know.'

"While we were changing, he noticed that the *shochet* had numbers on his arm. (These tattooed numbers were given to him free of charge at Auschwitz.) The young man couldn't seem to take his eyes off the numbers. When the *shochet* took off his pants to put on his jump suit, the Ph.D. candidate also noticed the *tzitzis* the *shochet* was wearing. Before he could say anything, the time had come for the *shechitah*. Quickly we tested out the pen. We lined up the six sheep and began slaughtering.

"The pen turned out to be of inferior design. A lot of work still remained to be done before sheep could be slaughtered on a commercial basis." Rabbi Wein continued, "We went back to take off the bloody suits and get dressed when the young Jewish man asked Reb Mendel, " 'Those numbers on your arm, where did you get them?' "

Tersely, the *shochet* answered, "Auschwitz."

"And what's that undershirt you wear?" He then pointed at his *tzitzis*, "You know, the large striped garment with the strings hanging from it?"

The total innocence behind these questions must have aroused the *shochet* because he stopped dressing and straightened up to look the young Jew squarely in the face. With his jump suit trailing behind him, he gathered up his front *tzitzis* with the tattooed arm and walked over to the young Jew. Sadly, he pointed with his free hand at the 'oddities,' the strings and the numbers. Slowly and deliberately he explained, "This garment is called '*tzitzis*.' If you knew what the garment meant, then you would also know what the numbers meant." Shaking his head mournfully from side to side, the *shochet* turned back to his pile of clothes without waiting for a reply.

The young man had been told something important about his nature but, alas, he had been kept in the dark too long about his Jewishness.

Feeling so uninformed about himself made him very uneasy, so he blurted out defensively, "Well, so what if I don't know what your garment is called; it has nothing to do with me, does it, these *tzitzis?*" Rabbi Schwartz tucked his shirt inside his pants and sighed to himself.

Probably in another setting, Rabbi Wein would have taken pains to explain the meaningfulness of the *shochet's* charge but in that bloody barn he chose not to say a word. He also felt the young man was too upset to listen anyway. The young Jew just turned away and stood staring at his sheep pen. The sheep lay there bleeding as the flies dipped into their wounds, and he was figuring how to rebuild the enclosure.

Rabbi Wein concludes, "We finished dressing in silence. There was not much more to say as we left the barn to head for home and I never found out if the young man got his doctorate."

> *Holocaust survivors today still feel the need to bear witness, to describe the unbelievable. In a recent New York Times book review of Ida Fink's survivor story, "The Journey," Primo Levi explains why he had not removed the number the Nazis tattooed on his arm. He said is was so that strangers would ask what it stood for and know that such a thing really happened.*
>
> *In this story, a young Jewish stranger did not know what the numbers meant, and he was ignorant of the mitzvah of tzitzis. But the connection between the numbers and the stripes can never be erased from our cultural heritage. Even the uninformed sense this truth.*

The Humane Society Strikes Again

"Humane societies are historically anti-Semitic. The Prophet Hoshea (13:2) says: 'Those who are willing to kill man, want to kiss the calf.' That is the animal lovers' warped point of view. It's better that man should die than that we should hurt animals.

"I don't mean to demean animals," Rabbi Wein says. "The Torah prohibits anyone from causing animals pain or suffering. But things have gotten out of hand. According to the New York City Bureau of Vital Statistics, in this year alone 2,000 citizens were victims of homicide. Every four hours somebody gets killed in New York City. No one ever protests. But to use animals for medical research provokes demonstrations.

"Last week a dog got loose in the subway and for over three hours the Transit Authority was trying to avoid killing the dog. All subways under the East River were stopped. Trains were rerouted. Eventually the confused animal ran under the wheels of a train in Brooklyn. The animal lobby blamed the Transit Authority for cruelty to animals and the next day the District Attorney's office was called in to investigate the case. An official city investigation was the result of one stray dog.

"Every day in Harlem, or Crown Heights, or South Ozone Park, innocent people are shot on the street corners in drive-by murders and cold-blooded assassinations and no one says a word. But Heaven forbid you should wear a beaver coat on Madison Avenue, or treat a rat with an experimental drug!

"Kosher *shechitah* is always under pressure in the United States. There was a bill passed in the United States around 1960 to outlaw inhumane slaughtering of animals. However, Jewish ritual animal slaughter was termed an 'exception' to this law. The only reason kosher *shechitah* is allowed is because we have been granted an exemption. If it weren't for an amendment written into the *Cruelty to Animals Bill* our method of *shechitah* would be outlawed.

"Hubert Humphrey, the Senator from Minnesota, and a great friend of the Jews, was responsible for saving *shechitah* in the United States. He used his political power to push the 'exception' for *shechitah* in the *Cruelty to Animals Bill*. But the amendment doesn't say that kosher slaughter is humane; it's just exempted from the bill.

"No one has ever explained how in the non-kosher slaughter houses they manage to be humane when they kill the animals. In the non-kosher slaughter houses a stun gun is held to the head of the animal. It is stunned and then shot dead with a bullet to the head. This is reputed to be humane, but in kosher slaughter houses slitting the animal's throat is considered inhumane. Nobody can explain the difference to me, nor has any animal ever returned from the dead to testify which method was more enjoyable. There's no nice way to kill; it hasn't been invented yet. The antiseptic, aesthetic style of killing has eluded us. In the slaughterhouses it's a bloody, gory mess.

"In Sweden and Switzerland, *shechitah* is not legally permitted. Do the slaughterhouses there smell differently from kosher ones elsewhere? When I worked for the O.U. we always were looking to improve our methods. We intended to appease the pro-animal lobbies without violating the rituals demanded of us by the Torah. But there's no nice way to kill an animal. There's just no way around this — if you want to have lamb chops, you have to slaughter sheep."

Food, Glorious Food

Jews have always been fascinated by all aspects of eating. A remarkably large portion of the *halachah* deals with the laws of eating: how to wash before eating, the blessings before and after eating, and the laws of kashruth. In addition, eating is a major element in the celebration of each holiday. On Passover, for instance, we are commanded to consume four items: *matzah*, *morror* (bitter herbs), four cups of wine, and in the days of yore, the *korban pesach* (Paschal lamb).

Even Jews who, unfortunately, have lost their tradition have not lost their involvement with food. It is estimated that 40% of people who eat Chinese food are Jewish. In his years as a rabbi in Miami Beach, Rabbi Wein found that in the kosher, Orthodox hotels food was inordinately important to the clientele. "They couldn't get enough of it," he says. "In Yiddish, there's a famous folk-saying that at Pesach '. . . people come for the *knaidlach* (soup balls), not the *Haggadah* (Passover story).'"

According to the Rabbi, "Kosher Expo is a negative example of our involvement with eating. It is regrettable that such phenomena as 'Glatt Cruise' and 'This Can't be Shrimp' blur our vision and prevent us from focusing on the true purpose of food. Eating is an opportunity to sanctify God, He wants us to enjoy the food He has provided us so we can continue to serve Him. Therefore, we should be careful to resist the blandishments of a fast food, drive-in, eat-on-the-run culture. When a Jew eats *l'shma*, (for the name — for the sake of heaven) he is doing something holy, and when he doesn't he is '*m'tamtaim es halev*,' stopping up his heart, and over a length of time it diminishes his potential as a Jew to do good.

❀ ❀ ❀

"After three generations of eating shrimp, the fourth generation is not going to feel very Jewish, and, consequently, is not going to give much money to Jewish causes. That's a rule. It's like eating cholesterol. You can enjoy eating tasty foods, but they stop-up the arteries. Non-kosher food stops-up the spiritual arteries.

"Only 18% of Jews give money to the U.J.A. What happened to the other 82%? Less than 20% of American Jews have visited Israel. Why? Stopped-up hearts. These are the Jewish actuarial tables. It takes a hundred years, but it finally stops-up the Jewish heart, too."

3
Kosher Money

Kosher money is harder to find than kosher food.

Kosher Money

At the age of 46, in 1928, Mr. Frankel, (a fictitious name) a wealthy labor lawyer in New York City, suffered a massive heart attack. After examining him, the doctors said that if he continued working at his present pace he had five years to live. His heart was too frail to last longer.

He decided to retire and enjoy the remainder of his life in Florida. He purchased annuities that would support him comfortably for the next forty years, and moved into a beautiful home on Pine Tree Drive in the Miami Beach area. Slowly, he settled into a peaceful routine of piety, giving charity to Jewish causes. A great *baal tzedakah*, his favorite charity was the Ponevezhe Yeshiva.

The first time Rabbi Wein met him was when Mr. Frankel was eighty-four years old in 1966. The Rabbi recalls, "I was a Rav in a synagogue in Miami Beach and Mr. Frankel was one of my most stalwart congregants. Still spry and marvelously alert, he was a delightful senior who helped set the standards for charitable endeavors in our synagogue. One day he called me in for a visit.

"His housekeeper ushered me into his dining room where he revealed his life had taken an ominous turn.

"Rabbi, I'm now eighty-five years old, and a terrible thing has happened to me. I've outlived my income. When I was a younger man, the doctors only gave me five years to live, so to be on the safe side I bought forty years of annuities. Now all my doctors are dead and my annuity has been spent. I've lived within my means but beyond my years."

Sadly, he reported that he would have to sell his house and let his housekeeper go. "I'll have to change my whole standard of living. For the last five years I've been selling off my assets to meet expenses. The social security checks came in handy, but now it's not enough. I'll sell this house and move back to Teaneck."

As he spoke, Rabbi Wein thought about how Choni Hamaagel, the Talmudic Rip Van Winkle, had awoken after seventy years to encounter an alien world in which he knew no one. The Sage, Rava, commented on his story, "Give me a friend or give me death." He had outlived all his friends and found himself estranged in an alien society.

Frankel hadn't been sleeping all these years. He was still a dynamo, actively involved in the central concerns of his life.

Rabbi Wein knew Rabbi Yosef Kahaneman, the Ponevezher

Rav. The Rav had been the main benefactor of Frankel's charity over the years. He was coming into town the following week on a fundraising trip. "Mr. Frankel, I have an idea. Don't sell the house yet. I think we may be able to work this out."

When the Ponevezher Rav came into town, Rabbi Wein took him over to Frankel's home. Rabbi Kahaneman listened to his plight intently. He knew that Frankel had probably given over a million dollars to his Yeshiva, both when it was in Europe and now in its reincarnated state in Israel. "This can't happen," he said, bewildered, "this can't be."

Rabbi Wein, trying to be helpful, began to explain the financial facts of life, but the venerable Rabbi was way ahead of him. "Mr. Frankel, for forty-five years you supported Torah, now Torah is going to support you."

Rav Kahaneman made a decision that startled Rabbi Wein. On the spot, he put Mr. Frankel on the payroll of the Ponevezhe Yeshiva. For the remaining two years of his life, Mr. Frankel made his living working as a "fundraiser" for the yeshiva he had supported all his life. As they left his house, the Ponevezher Rav said to Rabbi Wein, "*Tzedakah* (charity) is a two-way street. It benefits the giver as well as the receiver. We'll just redirect some of his money back to him."

Before his death, Frankel requested that he be buried in a very simple service and in his will left the remainder of his estate to the Ponevezher Yeshiva, returning *tzedakah* money once more to needy Torah scholars.

The Slap Heard Round the World

Rav Kook was an activist, and on many occasions he felt it necessary to assert his authority in the community even if he had to do it physically. In his synagogue in Boisk he would make his rounds in the morning pacing the aisles during morning prayers, checking the *tefillin* of each congregant. He was a stickler for proper placement of the head *tefillin;* if it was off to the side even slightly, he would adjust it.

Not everyone was happy with Rav Kook's exacting standards. And so it happened that once a man in his early twenties was wearing his *tefillin* slightly askew and when the Rav came to adjust it, the young man roughly pushed his hand away. Stunned momentarily, Rav Kook slapped him across the face.* (In Lithuania, the tradition was that the Rav could slap disrespectful congregants — "A custom I have been sorely tempted to introduce to Monsey," comments Rabbi Wein.) The slap left more than a sting on the cheek. When the Rav slapped someone it was the supreme stigma and usually forced the synagogue member to leave town. And so it was; after this incident the man quietly departed for America.

Many years later, in 1924, after Rav Kook had moved to the Holy Land and been appointed the Chief Rabbi of Israel, he traveled to the United States along with Rabbi Meir Don Plotsky and Rabbi Moshe Mordechai Epstein to raise funds for the yeshivas in *Eretz Yisroel.* The three great Rabbis were treated to a reception at the Waldorf Astoria Hotel welcoming them to New York. Numerous guests lined up for the privilege of personally greeting each of these giants.

---

* Rabbi M. Z. Neyriyahu in his book about Rav Kook reports this "potch" as a rebuke for mistreating a talmid chacham. Rabbi Wein heard it the way it is recorded here.

When one middle aged man reached Rav Kook, he asked him, "Rebbe, do you remember me?"

Rav Kook looked at him closely and said, "No."

"Rebbe, don't you remember? From Boisk? I didn't have *tefillin* on properly and you came to fix it and I pushed you away and you slapped me and I had to leave town."

"Yes," Rav Kook said, "Now I remember you."

"Rebbe, you might not believe this, but I thank you for what you did," the man said with a smile. "When I left Boisk in shame I had nowhere to go, so I came to America. I started a business here and the Lord blessed me with a great deal of success." The man bent over and kissed the Rav's hand, pulled out a check and left him with a large donation.

This was but one example of Rav Kook's power over his *Kehillah*, a power that spanned continents.

> *According to Rabbi Wein, in Europe every Rav had the ultimate weapon which he could use to control his congregants, the "potch" (the slap). In America all we can do to gain the attention of our members is to remind them we're going to say the hesped (funeral oration) over their coffin.*

We Don't Believe in Ourselves

Theodore Herzl died of heart disease in 1904, at the age of forty-four. During his career as President of the World Zionist Organization, he never took a salary and paid for all his expenses out of his own pocket. He died penniless. His wife and four children appealed to the Zionists for money on which to live. It was agreed that Herzl's family could not remain destitute and the leaders asked their membership for funds to assist them. In a very short time, three million dollars were raised and the leadership searched for a secure investment that would guarantee an income for Herzl's family.

Many ideas were considered and the Zionist leadership selected the 4% thirty-year bonds of the Austro-Hungarian Empire. This bond represented the safest and most secure paper in central Europe. Backing the bond was the good faith and will of the strongest, most powerful empire on the Continent. In 1906, this assured the family members a substantial income for the rest of their lives.

Eight years and one world war later, the Austro-Hungarian Empire had ceased to exist. The bonds which were supposed to support Herzl's children became worthless. The committee is not to be faulted for making what turned out to be a terrible investment. That would be asking them to see into the future. What is curious is the fact that in the minutes of the committee which reviewed investments, not one member chose to consider the long-term bonds of the Zionist organization itself, the Keren Hayesod and Jewish National Fund. Both of these bonds are still good and for the ninety years of their existence have not missed a payment.

> *We have the best product in the world, the land of Israel, backed by the strongest Guarantor. Why don't we realize it?*

Unexpected Profits

El Al, whose name means "to the skies" in Hebrew, was founded in 1948 as a bare-bones carrier mainly to ferry Jewish refugees for the new nation of Israel, and is still government-owned. The airline ran into big problems early in the last decade and became notorious for poor service and frequent strikes by its 13 unions. In danger of failing, it was shut down for four months in 1983. The year before, El Al had hit rock bottom; it lost $100 million, and suffered a crippling series of strikes which ended in a walkout by its flight attendants who demanded a bigger cut from sales of duty-free goods. Under new President, Mr. Harlev, an ex-General in the Israeli Air Force, the fractious unions were brought under one umbrella organization and a third of the workers were dismissed. By 1986, El Al had turned around, showing a profit of $15.2 million and has been in the black since. The $24.2 million it earned in 1989 is its peak. Its debt has been reduced from $320 million to about $100 million.

In May 1991, *The New York Times* featured an article on El Al. The headline read, "In Adversity, El Al Shifts To Cargo And Turns A Profit." In the article, the company was lauded for doing the right thing at the right time. The *Times* is to be commended writing about Israel in a positive light. But it also does not mention a significant event that took place in that fateful year, 1984, when the airline began to cut its losses. In 1984 the airline stopped its flights on *Shabbos* and religious holidays. This has been its policy ever since.

They shut down twenty percent of their operation and inexplicably made more money than before. No one expects a secular American newspaper to make the connection between *Shabbos* and profit. Financial analysts are too scientific for that. But would American Jews believe that an airline which travels one day a week less would make more money than before?

We just don't believe in ourselves.

The Law of Increasing Returns

People who have a large family need more than a smaller family. Expansion makes the parents capable of enlarging the borders of their wealth; and if you play by the book, God will fill those wider borders with more wealth, making possible larger borders. The world looks at it differently: If you want to guarantee your wealth the world says you must have a small family. Malthus looked at the world differently from the Bible.

Hefsed Merubah

Does substantial monetary loss provide grounds for halachic leniency? This question is labeled in the Talmud as "hefsed merubah." Rabbis are conflicted about this issue; on the one hand, the Torah does not require superhuman sacrifices in all circumstances; on the other hand, nobody said keeping Torah mitzvos was always going to be easy.

Rabbi Wein tells the story of a man who was a mortgage broker. He owned a business which serviced mortgages too small for the giant firms to handle directly. One day he received a call from the president of his largest client, the Equitable Life Insurance Company. "Joe," he announced, "I am going to be in town on Tuesday and I'd like to meet with you. We're thinking about enlarging our small policy sector. What is a good time for you?"

Now, Joe was put on a spot. The festival of Succos was slated to begin on Tuesday and Joe wondered how this man would take the postponement. "Actually," he replied, "Tuesday is impossible for me."

"No problem, let's make it Wednesday," came the accommodating counter-offer.

Joe wished he hadn't said that, "You know, come to think of it, Wednesday is not very good either."

The President of Equitable became annoyed. "What do you mean?" he asked. "I am giving you two days from which to choose. You know, I don't fly to your town that often."

Joe decided to play it straight. "Let me explain. Perhaps you didn't know but I am an observant Jew and the holiday of Succos falls on Tuesday and Wednesday — my offices are closed on both days."

The President was incredulous. "Surely, you don't mean to tell me there is no one around your offices for two consecutive business days?"

Joe told him the truth, "That's our policy."

"But, what if there's an emergency? What if a vital call comes through? We deal in a service business and accessibility to our customers is of prime importance. Joe, if what you're telling me is so, then I'm going to have to reevaluate our whole relationship." With that the President hung up.

Joe attended synagogue that Succos as he did every other Succos. On Thursday morning, upon his return to the office, the first phone call he received was from the President.

"Joe, I flew into town on Tuesday and I checked you out. Sure enough, you were closed, so I did some other business. To tell you the truth, I was feeling pretty hot that you couldn't find time for me. Now, I don't know why I did this, but I stayed over and on Wednesday afternoon I called again. I was told by your service that you wouldn't be in until Thursday because of religious observance. Two whole days off when the rest of the world is doing business! Imagine that.

"In this day and age it's got to take a lot of conviction for someone to do that. Joe, I've changed my mind about you. I'm coming down next Friday to review our position. I think anyone who has the courage to stand up to the world and stay closed when everyone else is open is my kind of man. I think we're ready to expand in your direction. What do you say?"

"That sounds great. Friday morning is fine," gulped Joe, deeply grateful the President hadn't designated the days of *Shemini Atzeres* and *Simchas Torah*.

The two have enjoyed a cordial business relationship ever since.

Trump Cards

The students at Shaarei Torah were learning about money matters in one of the standard gemaras studied in yeshivas, Bava Metziah. One day Rabbi Wein's class examined the following issue: 'What is the market value of a shtar (written contract)?

According to the Talmudic commentator, the Nesivos, Rabbi Yaakov Lorbeerbaum, in marketing this paper obligation (shtar) the potential buyer must factor in an important consideration: Does the borrower have the financial ability to pay off his loan? If not, he may well default on the loan rendering the paper worthless. According to the

> *Nesivos, in acquiring paper of a poorly financed debtor, one must discount the shtar more heavily than when acquiring paper issued by a debtor with a superior credit record and standing.*

Rabbi Wein uses his vast repertoire of stories to illustrate how credit can affect the value of a contract. He tells of a friend who was running a decorating business working mostly with hotels. He had made a bid to decorate the new Donald Trump gambling casino and hotel, the Taj Mahal, in Atlantic City. After months of waiting, the news got back to him. He didn't win the right to decorate the entire hotel but he had won the bid to drape part of the main ballroom, an immense undertaking that would guarantee at least a half a million dollars profit to the firm.

The following week, before the businessman had a chance to hire additional staff and start ordering from his suppliers, Trump's purchasing agent called with terrible news. Mr. Trump canceled the commitment and decided to give the contract to someone else. He gave no reasons for the switch.

The thought of all that money slipping through his fingers was crushing news. The purchasing agent sensed his disappointment and sought to alleviate some of the pain by throwing him a much smaller bone. He gave him the contract to provide drapes for one of the smaller baccarat gambling rooms, which adjoined the mammoth main gambling hall. This contract was worth only $30,000.

What happened next was all over the front pages. After the building was erected, Trump, deep in debt, could no longer afford to pay any of the banks which had loaned him the money. The Taj Mahal declared insolvency and his creditors lined up to lay claim to what was left of the assets of the casino. At the end of the line stood the drapery man with his modest lien for decorating the small gambling room.

He called Rabbi Wein with the news. "Rabbi," he said, "am I lucky or what? I was preparing to spend $100,000 to buy special machines for this job. If I had won the large contract I would have been completely wiped out. Now I will only lose a couple thousand dollars."

"Isn't that fortunate?" The Rabbi said dryly.

"Just yesterday, I received a letter from Trump's lawyers," the businessman continued. "They wanted to know if I would take ten cents for every dollar he owes me so we can settle his debt. I took what I could get. Otherwise, who knows? I might get nothing!"

After regaling his class with that anecdote, Rabbi Wein returned to the Talmud. "This is exactly what the *Nesivos* is talking about," Rabbi Wein explained. "If the debtor can only pay a tenth of the debt then that is what the contract is worth. This *Gemara* (Talumdic passage) is talking about today's *Wall Street Journal*. Junk bonds! What is this paper really worth? And don't forget the Nesivos wrote this at a time when paper money did not exist."

Rabbi Wein scanned the room as he waxed philosophical. "The problem is that most people think that *Gemara* is *Gemara* and life is life. They do not realize that life is *Gemara* and *Gemara* is life."

If I Were a Rich Man

Rabbi Wein states that in Miami he learned about the value of money. He didn't make a lot of it there, "But, I certainly learned a great deal about it."

He tells this story about a man named Mr. Brill (this is a fictitious name). "One of my friends, a good Jew named Brill, had just sold a large kosher wine company, which he owned outright and debt-free, to the Borden Company for 37 million dollars. He took his money and invested it in government bonds.

"He was a man in his eighties and was always a big contributor to Jewish causes. It was a pleasure to do business with him; he was always so forthcoming. Once I brought a great Rabbi from Jerusalem to him to solicit funds for a venerable yeshiva to which he had always given generously in the past.

"Mr. Brill listened to the Rabbi explain that the yeshiva desperately needed a new dormitory and it needed operational money to fund the deficit, etc. He agreed to help out, took out his checkbook and wrote his donation. When the Rabbi took the check he saw the sum was substantially below the philanthropist's usual standards.

The Rabbi expressed his disappointment, "Did I say something wrong? You usually give so much more."

Mr. Brill tried to make him understand that it wasn't the Rabbi's fault, but now things had changed for him: "The last time you came I was still working and drawing down a salary. When I gave you last year I could afford to give, because it came from current income. Now, I don't have a job any more. I sold my business and when I give now it comes out of capital, so I have to watch it."

The Rabbi couldn't argue him out of his perception. If you think you're poor, you're poor.

If I Were a Rich Man #2

Last year, Rabbi Wein's friend, a lawyer, finally made it big. The law firm he works for made him a senior partner and rewarded him with a new Jaguar. Is there anything greater a Jewish boy could hope for? That night he drove home and parked it in front of his house. He didn't put it in the garage but on the street right in front of his house for the neighbors to see.

The next morning, the Monsey sanitation truck came to collect the garbage and while the men were doing their job they backed the truck right into the Jaguar and smashed it. Do you know what it is like to try to collect insurance on a Jaguar? He worked on it for six months straight. He couldn't do any law work, his home life was suffering, and he couldn't even eat because this insurance business was driving him crazy. It took three secretaries to get through to the top adjuster because anything over $30,000 needed special approval and the Jaguar was insured for $40,000 dollars.

One day, he walked over to Rabbi Wein and said, "Believe me, I'm never going to own a Jaguar again — the next car I buy is going to be a Plymouth. If the garbage truck totals it, it's all settled in four hours — Lee Iococca sends you the parts and you're back on the road by the weekend."

Rabbi Wein uses this incident to educate his students about the dangers of conspicuous consumption: "A Jewish boy doesn't need to drive a foreign car or live in a mansion. I am not proposing that people live in poverty, but what is important to understand is that life is not found in things. Things will betray you. One of our neighbors just moved into the community from Flatbush. He built a two million dollar French Normandy home and it's gorgeous — it's got a slate, mansard roof, thirty-foot ceilings, the finest appointments.

"The pity of it is that the man is depressed about the way things have turned out. His wife is scared to move around in the house. It's built way back in the woods and every time she hears something it scares her out of her wits because the thirty-foot ceilings amplify every little noise. She misses her friends in Brooklyn and can't wait for the next invitation to visit 'back home.' Her husband is worn down by the commute to his office in downtown New York City and on top of it all he's having a hard time selling his old house in Brooklyn. Lately he admits that he may have been too hasty in constructing such a baronial mansion. He is a sensitive man who is smart enough to understand the consequences of building such an edifice. 'I wanted to make a statement,' he says ruefully, 'but it's hard to live in statements.'"

Liquid Assets

A neighbor of Rabbi Wein was walking around his property late one afternoon. He looked so sad that Rabbi Wein thought something terrible had happened to him.

"Is there anything wrong with you? Can I be of any help?" the Rabbi asked.

"You can't help me," he said. "I need an investment counselor, Rabbi. I'm liquid two million dollars and I don't know where to put it — and it's driving me crazy."

Rabbi Wein thought: "He is walking around so dejected, one would think his two million dollars were owed rather than uninvested." The Rabbi then said to his distraught neighbor, "I hate to see people walking around in pain. Give it to me. I have a great investment record; my clients always profit. Give the money to the yeshiva, it'll be the best investment you'll ever make."

> "Torah is the best investment in the world," Rabbi Wein contends. "Look at the last five years. In 1987 the stock market crashed; in 1990 the bottom fell out of the real estate market; and lately the economy has gone into a tailspin. But my clients have always succeeded. I suggest only one major investment. That is the yeshiva. Over thousands of years no one has ever lost by investing in Torah."

※ ※ ※

A famous university recently published a study on the effects of winning the lottery. The purpose of the study was to determine if sudden wealth made any difference to the families of the winners.

The study indicated that lottery winners divorced more than average, were imprisoned more than average, and suffered more mental illness since they won their money. It was found that too much money could be a terrible burden causing more pain and damage to the social lives of the winners than to those who did not win.

As Rabbi Wein puts it, "Most of us would not reject lottery winnings, although we know instinctively that sudden wealth could destroy our lives."

※ ※ ※

A chain letter asks the recipient to pay a dollar to the ten people listed and add his name to the list and send copies of the letter to twenty of his friends. It promises that by the fifth cycle of letters he will receive over a million dollars.

There are sales organizations and buying clubs which operate on the principle of the chain letter. One is urged to sell products to friends and enlist them as representatives who then will sell the products to others. Each new salesperson pays commission to his predecessor. He, in turn, repeats the cycle enlisting his friends as sales personnel, and they kick back commissions to him because he is higher up on the pyramid.

It's an attractive proposal and holds great promise until one considers two things: First, the people forced to buy will most probably be friends and relatives. Second, it doesn't take very long (nine cycles of salespeople) for everyone on earth to become a salesperson. This means that if the program succeeds and the salespeople reach their goal, in a short space of time everyone on earth will be selling company products to company personnel and the market will be exhausted.

This is a perversion of the statement found in *Ethics of our Fathers,* "Spend your resources in order to acquire a friend." The pyramid corporation believes the opposite — it says "Sell your friends (coerce them into buying) in order to acquire resources."

Achdus Yisroel

Rabbi Wein feels very strongly about achdus Yisroel, unity amongst all Jews, and it's best to hear him talk about this topic without any interference.

"We (the Orthodox) tend to take pokes at 'U.J.A. Jews,' 'Israel Bond Jews,' even 'Federation Jews.' However, during the Gulf War, when I went on the El Al plane to Israel, who were my flight companions but these same Jews we sometimes look down upon. They were going into a war zone, and they were not going there to get something; they were going to give. When push comes to shove you don't ask what kind of Jew are you. We know that God did not make one extra Jew and we must stand together.

"Look at the *kiddush Hashem* (sanctification of God's name) that is involved with Operation Moses. The Israelis brought the Ethiopians out — 14,000 in one airlift — put them in homes, fed them, gave them clothes, and Hebrew lessons, all in the space of a day. Now that is something! What does the rest of the world do? What did the Greeks do to 3,000 ethnic Greeks living in Bulgaria who wanted to flee the chaos there and begged to come across the border to their homeland? The Greeks didn't let them in!

"The other week, Polish leader, Lech Walesa, was in Chicago raising money for the Polish people. At a fundraising dinner he appealed to the Polish community in Greater Chicago (close to a million people) to help his nation recover from communist rule. He raised $1,500,000; that works out to less than $2.00 for every Polish-American living in and around Chicago; believe me, that's not enough to save Poland."

Tremendous Opportunities

According to Rabbi Wein, we are being given tremendous spiritual opportunities in our time. He illustrates this by recounting a conversation he had with an old friend.

"I have a close friend in the midwest. He and I attended the same yeshiva, and now he's an expert in investments with a nationwide clientele. He's very, very successful.

"I once spoke in his town and afterwards I spent the night in his home. Naturally, we stayed up, reminiscing — until 12 o'clock at night. At that point I said I was quite tired; so I excused myself to go to bed. He said, 'All right, I've still got a few calls to make.'

"My ears perked up and I remarked, 'Calls to make! It's twelve midnight — who are you going to call?

" 'You don't understand,' my friend replied. 'I have some very important information to give a number of clients — absolutely great opportunities — I'll call them tonight, and when the market opens in the morning, they'll be ready. They'll appreciate the call.'

"You're going to call someone at twelve or one o'clock in the morning to tell them that?'

" 'What, are you crazy, Berel?' he replied. 'I'm telling you, this is business. That's why they stick with me. They know I'll call them at 3:00 in the morning and tell them, 'Hey — we can make money tomorrow!'

"So, I sat there and thought to myself — and I think to myself often — if I could be like him . . . and if I really believed the speeches that I make, then I would call my congregants also at one o'clock in the morning and tell them, 'Look, I've got a great *hachnosos-kallah* (charity for brides) for you — it's available in the morning! There's a *mitzvah* over here — a Jew we can help. We can save him. At the opening bell we can save him for sure.' But I'm afraid I'll wake them up and they'll be angry, so I don't call after 9:30 or 10:00. I look at it as a burden — and the Lord looks at it as an opportunity."

Rabbi Kaplan, the Wine Maker

The story is told that Rabbi Mendel Kaplan, *zt'l*, was often at odds with the administration of the yeshivas he worked in. He continually had to defend his European viewpoint to an American-born administration. In order to free himself of the financial constraints of being a hired hand, he entered into business. He felt that wine making best suited his abilities, so he rented a garage and set up what he hoped would be a successful winery. Perhaps he fancied himself a combination Rabbi and vintner like the fabled Rashi.

At any rate, his venture did not succeed. No matter how hard he tried, the business never took off. At times, it would show signs of succeeding but then for some reason would falter. After a major disappointment in his wine-making career he asked a friend for advice. His friend was consoling but told it to him straight.

"Reb Mendel," he explained, "from a technical point of view, there's nothing I can tell you that would improve your business. The product is first-rate; your management practices are sensible. However, I do see one thing you need to make you a success in this business."

Reb Mendel listened carefully, "Nu, what is it?"

His friend leveled with him. "It's your attitude. In order to be successful in business, you need to love to make money. It's not sufficient to make just a little money. You have to learn to love it."

Rabbi Mendel thought about what his friend had just said. Then he threw up his hands in a gesture of helplessness. His friend had hit home. He knew the truth when he heard it and wistfully agreed, *"Dos ken ich kain mal nisht lernen."* ("This, I will never be able to learn.")

A short while after this conversation took place, he closed his business and eventually moved to Philadelphia to become a Rabbi in the yeshiva there.

> People speak of Rabbi Kaplan fondly and with reverence. His influence still radiates in his graduates throughout the Torah world. (See Chapter Five, The Song of a Yeshiva).

Family Business

When his best pupil left Radun to get married, the Chofetz Chaim was afraid that his father-in-law would make him a partner in his business. The disciple protested that the fears of the Chofetz Chaim were unjustified.

Shortly after the wedding, though, the father-in-law pressured the young man to enter his business as a "junior" partner. Reluctantly, the newly married son-in-law took leave of his mentor to enter the world of business. "It's only temporary," he reassured the Chofetz Chaim. "I'll come right back to Radun."

For the next three months, the young man worked diligently at the side of his father-in-law. In that short span of time the father-in-law learned to rely on his good business sense and shrewd decision making. Confident of his son-in-law's abilities, he left the factory to him and went to England to expand the business.

As soon as he left, everything went wrong. There was trouble with the workers, the firm's main supplier went out of business and finally his top salesman quit, taking the best accounts with him.

For a veteran businessman, these events would have been severe. For the son-in-law they were calamitous. When the father-in-law heard what was going on he rushed home to assume control of the company. In an effort to cut costs, the father-in-law fired excess personnel, including his son-in-law.

Crestfallen, the *choson* (young married man) went back to the yeshiva. However, he felt terrible about his failure as a businessman and this affected his learning. The Chofetz Chaim spoke to him privately and gave him this penetrating analysis: "I know you are deeply hurt by your failure. You felt you could have made a fortune and in a short time you almost lost the entire business. That is certainly disappointing. But there's another way to look at it. You could have taken forty years of unsuccessful business dealings to fritter away such a sum of money. Here you did the whole thing in six months and got it over with quickly. You should be thankful. Now you are free to learn full-time once again. Welcome home."

Soon the young man recovered his zest for learning and became once again the outstanding disciple in the yeshiva. He now understood that for the Jew, Torah learning is the real "family business."

Warm Hands

The Chofetz Chaim gained access to many Jewish upper class homes. Once, in Moscow on a fundraising trip, the Chofetz Chaim was introduced to a powerful figure in the world of international finance, who had just been honored by the Czar. Although sympathetic to Jewish causes, he was not a traditionally observant Jew. After meeting the financier and exchanging a few pleasantries, the mogul wrote out a large check.

The Rabbi took the check and thanked him, folded it and put it away in his wallet. He then took the man's hand between his own two hands and held it for a long time.

"Such a warm and generous hand," He said, stroking it lightly. "It's too bad that it's going to burn in *gehinnom* (Hell)."

Legend has it that the financier became *shomer Shabbos* on the spot.

The Story of Two Wills

The ensuing two stories were the centerpiece of Rabbi Wein's sermon on the Shabbos before Yom Kippur 5752. They referred to the song "Haazinu," which Moshe related to the Jewish people on the day of his death. The people learned the song as witness to the contract that God forged with them. "The song was put into their mouths," the Torah says — "forcibly," Rabbi Wein adds. "If they don't remember how to be Jews, the gentiles will teach them terrible, inescapable lessons. If they do remember who they are and behave as Jews, they will be privileged to enjoy the special status of a Jew."

Will Number One:

Rabbi Wein described a will which involved a prominent Jewish lawyer who was President of a large Reform synagogue in a suburban Michigan town. This man married a non-Jewish woman and had several children. His father-in-law was one of the wealthiest gentiles in Michigan, and the two families enjoyed an idyllic relationship. The Jewish lawyer invited his in-laws to his home on the major Jewish Holidays. The father-in-law invited his son-in-law and his daughter and his grandchildren to his home for Christmas and Easter. On Thanksgiving they alternated. This was the environment in which the grandchildren grew up.

When the wealthy grandfather passed away, his last will and testament was read before the entire family. It revealed that he excluded his grandchildren from the will. He cited the fact that they were his "Jewish" grandchildren and under no circumstances was any of his estate to be given to Jews. His "Jewish" grandchildren were to be given nothing.

The news was received with disbelief by the lawyer's family. "What kind of relationship did we really have all these years?" The lawyer felt utterly betrayed and decided to challenge the will in the courts.

He based his argument on the fact that the will specifically denied any money to his children because they were Jewish. He knew that, *halachically*, Jewish identity is matrilineal, carried on through the mother. Since his wife was a non-Jew, his children were not Jewish and he argued they could not be denied inheritance because of their Jewish identity. He brought a rabbi into court who testified that according to traditional Judaism the lawyer's children were not considered to be Jewish.

The judge who heard the case knew a little about the nature of American Judaism and queried the Jewish lawyer.

"Are you a traditional Jew?"

"If you mean," the lawyer answered, "am I an Orthodox Jew? the answer is no. I am a Reform Jew."

"What do Reform Jews consider the children of a Jewish man and a gentile woman?" the judge asked.

The President of the temple told the judge the way it was, "Such offspring would be called Jewish by the congregation. Most couples in my own temple are intermarried and we, of course, acknowledge the Jewishness of our children."

The judge heard the testimony and concluded that if the lawyer really considered his children to be Jewish then his late father-in-law was justified in identifying them as such. He ruled that the exclusion in the will was a legitimate right of the deceased. "If Jews think of your children as Jewish," he reasoned, "should the gentiles be given less credence for thinking the same?"

❦ ❦ ❦

Will Number Two:

When Rabbi Wein was a Rav in Miami Beach, the principal of the Miami Beach Day School was trying to expand on the success of his school and create a *mesivta* (high school). He formed a school board and asked Rabbi Wein to head up the fundraising committee. It was estimated that 400,000 dollars would be needed to purchase a site and construct the building. The board identified twenty men in the synagogue community who could well afford to donate $20,000 and a committee set out to raise the money. When the board members got to the home of one of the wealthiest men, they were met with a blaze of invective.

The man went into a tirade, "Who asked you to come here tonight? I certainly didn't."

The principal, who was part of this committee recalled, "It was as if we insulted the man by asking him to contribute."

"What makes you think that a *mesivta* is needed here? Most of the boys want to go to Miami Beach High School," he fumed. "Don't ever ask me for money for this project." He ranted on but before his rage got totally out of hand the group decided to leave. As they left they could hear him yelling, "I don't need a *ner tamid*, (eternal light which hangs by the ark). I don't need another plaque. Nothing! The school won't work. Not a dime, not a single dime."

The man's appraisal of the interest in Jewish secondary education was accurate. Rabbi Wein verifies that, "After the yeshiva was built the Rabbis had a very hard time recruiting a dozen ninth-graders to begin the school, and the struggle to maintain enrollment continued for three years."

The man's words hurt the spirits of the fundraising team a great deal: "You're mistaken if you believe I'll throw my money away." Those words echoed in the principal's brain and he wondered if the other potential donors would also answer with such bitterness. Another month of fundraising, however, proved that this man was the exception to the rule. The other respondents were much more positive. Still, the principal could not figure out why he rejected the project so bitterly?

The event happened twenty years ago and recently Rabbi Wein received a telephone call from the principal in Miami. "He is now retired," Rabbi Wein reported, "but we still keep in touch and he had some news about the school. The same *gvir* (wealthy citizen) died before the summer and last week they finished probating his estate. The principal said, 'The high school and I were mentioned in the will in a very long and detailed paragraph.' He continued, 'This man left the Miami *mesivta* $150,000. He stated that from the time I asked him for a donation years ago, it had been on his mind. He watched the progress of the school with interest and recently he benefited personally from the high school when he married off his granddaughter to a fine Miami *Mesivta* graduate.'

Through the years, the retired principal reported, "He'd seen the value of the school and now he wanted to make things right. 'Hopefully,' the will read, 'this bequest will atone for the first refusal.'"

The principal admitted to Rabbi Wein that he was totally surprised by the posthumous legacy but upon reflecting was able to figure it out.

"The will gave me an insight into the man's anger during that memorable tirade. The man was furious because he really wanted to give and was guilty for not being able to do so and the conflict was driving him wild. The more he tortured himself, the angrier became his rejection. Thank God, his wrath finally abated and he was able to give."

> "In conclusion," Rabbi Wein says, "Jewish guilt goes a long way. He really wanted to give when he was first solicited. Every Jew wants to give. Every Jew wants to play an important role in spreading Torah, but sometimes our brains get in the way. We reason, 'It doesn't make sense. It's too narrow. It's

medieval. It will make the boy less competitive.' Our rationalizations prevent us from giving. But the Jew is not a rejecting person. His neshoma (soul) says, 'Give.' It says, 'Build.' It counsels him, 'Do.' And for twenty-five years this man struggled until he could deny it no longer. He heard the song of Haazinu — that special Jewish melody that was placed in his mouth with loving insistence over 3,000 years ago. We can't resist the appeal of the Divine. Even if it takes twenty-five years to recall the words, the melody lingers on. Two wills, two legacies."

The $28,000 Coffin

Rabbi Wein is fond of asking, "How will it look fifty years from now? 500 years from now?" Perspective means a lot to him; every decision we make affects generations to come, for instance: "Who should we marry? What school is right for our kids? What occupation should we pursue? In this vignette, Rabbi Wein explores the question, "How will it look at the funeral?"

"When I was a Rav in Miami Beach I got to meet many wealthy people. It's the nature of the place. One of the wealthiest Jews lived just outside of Miami Beach. He owned real estate, supermarket chains, television stations and almost everything else worth owning was in his grasp. He was so wealthy he bought a whole island on Biscayne Bay on which he built an enormous home. At the end of a private causeway that connected him to the mainland he erected an electronically controlled cast iron gate that was fifteen feet high. Short of an amphibious assault by the Sixth Fleet no one gained access to his home. Needless to say, he was rarely visited by Jewish solicitors.

"When he started to attend our synagogue, we became friendly and I noticed that as the years passed he became more observant. He also became very charitable and used to give me about $10,000 every year to distribute anonymously to charities in the Miami Beach area. One day, this powerful and wealthy man made the mistake of dying, so the family called me up to preside at the funeral and make all the religious arrangements.

"At the funeral home in South Miami Beach the undertaker wanted to sell the widow a very gaudy casket that cost $28,000. It was made of highly polished brass and the interior was tufted in satin and trimmed with real mink piping. Burled, black walnut handles graced its outside. I don't know how to describe the overall design but it looked so inviting, I thought, if it had a motor I would have driven it out of the showroom.

"I discussed the matter with the family and told them that such a casket was not 'al pi halachah' (in accordance with Jewish law). Jews were not supposed to be buried in such sumptuous coffins. As far as burial was concerned, Jewish law was clear: opulence was to be shunned and a simple, inexpensive ritual was the preferred mode. So the family agreed that he should be buried in a plain pine box.

"When I conveyed their decision to the undertaker, he protested strongly, 'How can you do that to this man? He was a captain of industry! He was a corporate giant who was worth millions!'

"I answered him softly, 'The truth of the matter is that the man wanted to be buried *al pi halachah*. He did not want to be buried any other way. According to our tradition, 'Dead is dead,' and he understood this.'

"The mortician returned to his primary sales pitch, 'How will it look at the funeral? Half of Miami Beach is going to attend. They're going to hear the departed praised as a great Jewish-American leader and successful businessman. He was a great man who lived his life in grandeur; it's only fitting that he be buried in grandeur. He deserves better than a pine box.'

"I could sense the surviving family sway toward the mortician's flowery appeal. I knew they didn't want to 'shortchange' the memory of their patriarch. The eldest son turned to me and was about to say something when I launched a counter-offensive, 'You all know the biography of Moses Montefiore, the great Jewish financier and philanthropist, don't you?'

" 'Yes,' they said, of course they'd heard of him, faintly recalling the great nineteenth century figure who did so much for Israel and the Jewish people. One could see that their memory of this legendary figure needed refreshing. I decided to reacquaint them with Jewish-European history in the latter part of the last century.

" 'Moses Montefiore was a legend in his own time. He married into the Rothschild family and became so successful trading stocks and European currencies that by the time he was forty he had amassed a vast fortune which rivaled the wealth of his in-laws, the Rothschilds. Then, at the height of his powers, in mid-career, instead of continuing to build his wealth, he retired from the world of commerce and devoted himself entirely to the service of the Jewish people. Now this is the part that may interest you.' I checked my small audience quickly and found them all to be curious about the man. Even the undertaker was mildly interested as he absentmindedly buffed the brass casket with his handkerchief.

" 'One of the famous stories regarding him was that every night before retiring, he would descend to his basement, and don his *tachrichim* death shrouds, white linen garments, and lie down in the coffin he had prepared for himself, a plain pine box. He did this routine every night of his adult life and I think he lived till the ripe age of 104. In his will he left instructions that they bury him, *'al pi halachah,'* in the pine box he used to lie in during his life. He died as he lived, *'al pi halachah.'*

"The undertaker had stopped burnishing the expensive casket and yawned audibly. I moved to my conclusion.

" 'Certainly,' I began, 'the deceased lived a grand and opulent lifestyle. His accomplishments in the business world were stupendously successful. His charity work was notable for its scale as well as for the discretion in which it was conducted. However, at the end of his life he expressed a desire to come closer to traditional Judaism. He felt an affinity for halachah that grew continuously. He came to our synagogue regularly and was happy in his endeavor. I feel it is our duty to bury him as a traditional Jew. To me that would be a fitting way to conclude his affairs here on earth and prepare him for the world to come. Believe me, I know the deceased would not want a grander coffin than the one chosen by Sir Moses Montefiore.'

"I stepped back and stood in front of the $28,000 box. I folded my hands and waited, all the while looking solemnly at the ground. After a few seconds, the undertaker emitted a low sigh and shrugged his shoulders. The relatives seemed to acquiesce and stood mournfully silent. My invocation of the life of Sir Moses Montefiore had carried the day.

"The mortician recovered weakly. 'Now I've got simpler caskets back there.' He pointed halfheartedly to the other, distant side of the showroom. The salesman in him wouldn't quit but I think he knew he had met his match in the legendary Sir Moses. He marched up the aisle with the family in tow behind him. As they trailed off they thanked me for my advice. The $28,000 casket shone mutely in their wake. Someone less worthy would lie in it."

4

An Immortal People

Mark Twain: "The Egyptian, the Babylonian, and the Persian rose, filled the planet with sound and splendor, then faded to dream stuff and passed away; the Greek and the Roman followed, and made a vast noise, and they are gone; other prophets have sprung up and held their torch high for a time, but it burned out, and they sit in twilight now, or have vanished. The Jew saw them all, beat them all, and is now what he always was, exhibiting no decadence, no infirmities of age, no weakening of his parts, no slowing of his energies, no dulling of his alert and aggressive mind. All things are mortal but the Jew; all other forces pass, but he remains. What is the secret of his immortality?"

"Concerning the Jews" republished in The Complete Essays of Mark Twain; Doubleday, New York. 1963, page 249.

An Immortal People

ight years ago, in Rabbi Wein's yeshiva, Shaarei Torah, a Russian student was admitted into the senior year class. The boy's father, newly arrived from the Soviet Union, brought his son in, deposited him in his classroom and then disappeared.

Rabbi Wein didn't have a chance to meet his father until the end of the school year. The son did very well and when the term ended, at graduation ceremonies Rabbi Wein finally had a chance to talk with the father. He remembers him as a Jew who knew very little about his background. "He knew nothing; couldn't read a word of Hebrew; was not observant — nothing." Rabbi Wein asked him why he brought his son into a yeshiva.

"I'll tell you, Rabbi," the man said. "When we came here to the United States, both my son and I were not circumcised; we did not have a *bris*. Not only that, but I was determined that we were not going to be circumcised, because I remember in our town in Russia, when I was a boy, the Nazis came into town and ordered all the men of the village to stand in the center of the town and take off their clothes. When we were naked we were forced to raise our hands over our heads and march one by one in front of their guns. Every man who was circumcised was shot right on the spot. Therefore, I resolved to hide my Jewishness as much as possible — who needed it?

"There is an organization in our area," the man continued, "called Bris Avraham, which makes *brissin* for Russian Jews and they called me many times to get me to have a *bris* done. They're very aggressive and kept on pressuring me. They told me it wouldn't cost anything, that it wouldn't hurt, and that it was medically safe. They kept calling and coming to my door, so finally I gave in and both my son and I went to have a *bris*.

"After the bris, I enrolled my son in your yeshiva because I figured when they take him out to be shot he should at least know why they're going to kill him."

Rabbi Wein likes to explain that we can run from our destinies but we can't escape. "The last train to Auschwitz contained only Jews who had converted to Christianity, or whose parents had converted to Christianity. What a tragedy! To live like a *goy* and die like a Jew."

> Rabbi Wein: "On Rosh Hashannah, we listen to the sound of the shofar — the shofar is the sound of the ram's horn at Sinai. When we hear that sound we

are trapped by it — like the ram in the thicket by the akaidah (Issac's sacrifice), our horns are entrapped by the sounds of Jewish destiny and we can't escape our fate."

Comrade Yaakov

A Russian Jew emigrated to Monsey a few months ago. Over a hundred years old, he is an observant man who had lived through the entire communist debacle from the Czar through to Yeltsin! What an incredible testimony to the sheer willpower, determination, and stubborness of Jews who were cultivated in the heart of Mother Russia. However, equally as remarkable is his eighty-year-old daughter, who takes care of him now. All her years in Russia, she chose to remain single. When asked why, she answered: "I didn't want my father to be *mechutan* (related by marriage) to Esau."

Prisoners of Zion and their Dreams

Rabbi Shimon Grilius, a former refusenik, is now working with an organization called Shvut Ami. They are involved in the spiritual welfare of the Russian immigrants in Israel. At a Monsey parlor meeting, he recounted what it was like to be a Jew in the "University of Siberia."

He showed us the shirt he was issued by the KGB. It was a simple cotton smock open at the neck and coarsely finished on the inside. Grilius explained that it was just wide enough at the top so that the Siberian winds could penetrate easily. The crude, fibrous underside kept the wearer uncomfortable all the time. "Such is the cruelty of our oppressors," he said unemotionally. "The itching kept me awake for months."

He continued: "After Mendelevitch (a fellow prisoner) was assigned to my camp, we joined the same work details. When we saw that they didn't mind us working together we became inseparable. We talked Torah all the time — as much of it as we knew. He had a book of *Tehillim* (Psalms) with him and we would take turns memorizing it. Every three hours, with the changing of the guards, we would be let outside in the fresh air for a twenty-minute break.

"Sometimes, we had to shovel our way outside because the doorway was blocked with snow. Once outside we would tell each other our dreams. Mendelevitch would announce to me that we must emigrate to Israel. There we would marry Israeli women and have many children. 'Shimon,' he said, 'now, we are only skin and bones; we are rags! But, one day we will return to our land. We will marry and grow our own roots with the help of God.'

"With the help of God, his vision has been fulfilled. In 1975, Mendelevitch and I were released and, thank the Almighty, since then I have been privileged to have many children. We have made seven *bris milahs*. Who would have thought?"

Shimon Grilius stood before us, and in simple Hebrew explained his life. The words of this soft-spoken man made us cry, but the strength of his commitment signaled to us that there is something going on now that is unfolding, simply and powerfully, before our eyes. And it is irresistible. Can anyone stand in its way?

Mendelevitch, the Refusenik

"Compared to Mendelevitch, I am an amoeba." (Rabbi Wein's self-appraisal came after reading Yosef Mendelevitch's book 'Mivtzah: Chasuna,' a record of his eleven years in a Siberian labor camp. Here follows a short excerpt from the book, only available in Hebrew, that so impressed Rabbi Wein.

While he was in the work camp for the refuseniks, Mendelevitch decided to make a *kipah* (*yarmulka* or Jewish head covering) for himself. When the handmade *kipah* was finished, he wore it all the time. The KGB colonel in charge of the work camp saw him wearing his *kipah* and threatened him. "If you don't take that thing off, I'm going to kill you," he said. In order to intimidate Mendelevitch he flicked open the flap of his pistol holster.

Mendelevitch calmly informed him, "If you're going to kill me, do so; but I'm not afraid of you and I'm not going to take off my *kipah*."

The KGB couldn't afford to kill him; they wanted him to die, but they couldn't take the chance of killing him themselves. The Colonel was so astounded by his refusal to take off his skullcap that he screamed at him, "Aren't you afraid of death?"

Mendelevitch answered him, "I'm not afraid of death because I know that death comes from the hands of the Creator." He took a deep breath before going on: "Therefore, I'm not frightened of it. But you think that death comes at the hands of Brezhnev and therefore you are in terror of it."

They never were able to divest him of that *kipah*.

Chapter 4: An Immortal People

Trotsky's Grandson

"Trotsky, Lev Davidovitch (1879-1940), a Russian politician whose real name was Bronstein, was born in Elizavetgrad, the son of middle-class Jews . . . . He was the leader of . . . a party of social democrats and soon joined the Bolshevik party. He played a significant role in organizing the Bolshevik revolution. Trotsky was the most important Communist figure in the Russian delegation during the negotiation of the Brest-Litovsk peace treaty."

(Encyclopedia Britannica)

Rabbi Lev Bronstein, a direct descendant of Lev Trotsky, is a head of a kolel (Rosh Kolel) in Jerusalem.

One *Shabbos*, as Rabbi Wein stood outside synagogue wishing his members a good *Shabbos*, an elderly woman approached him.

"Rabbi," she said, "this is the first time in my life that I have ever been to a synagogue. I want to thank you for the wonderful service and your inspiring sermon. I would like to tell you a bit about my background. I arrived from the Soviet Union seven months ago where my family was a model of the communist ideal. We were taught to reject God and believe only in the powers of man, science, and technology. My father was one of the original members of the Communist Party. Lenin was party member number one; Trotsky was number two; my father was number six.

"I spoke with him just before he died and his final words to me were: 'I guess we can say the experiment has failed.'"

Rabbi Wein was struck by the story.

"Imagine," he said. "Her father spent his whole life — ninety years! — to build a future on a false dream, on a system destined for failure. 'I guess we can say the experiment has failed.' What shall we say about our system? Our Torah is not an experiment that will fail; it is a proven success. They waste a lifetime trying to create a utopia that cannot exist, all the while ignoring the *eitz hachaim* (tree of life) of the Torah."

Pesach in Chernobyl

In April, 1986, around Pesach time, the Russian nuclear facility in the Ukraine malfunctioned. In a disastrous near-meltdown, the city of Chernobyl was destroyed. A vast area was polluted by fallout and abandoned by the civilian population. A few months later, in a major policy decision, the Russian Army was ordered to withdraw its forces from Afghanistan. Two years later, in the wake of these major reversals, the dismantling of the Communist Empire commenced without a shot being fired.

At the same time an unprecedented airlift took place — 900 Russian Jews were flown daily from Russia to resettle in the land of Israel. By the spring of 1992, 350,000 Russian Jews had emigrated to Israel. Is there any connection between these events or are they only random occurrences?

Lord Immanuel Jacobowitz, then Chief Rabbi of England, offered this explanation: In a godless country, even the materialists need an ideal to live for. The idealism of Soviet Communism was centered on the twin gods of science and technology. In Chernobyl, the Russian gods melted down and the citizenry was stripped of its belief system. According to the Lord

> Rabbi, "Once their gods were discredited, the country itself started to crumble."
>
> One of Rabbi Wein's congregants shared her insights with us a week after Chernobyl. Her words proved to be prophetic. The following is my own vignette, not Rabbi Wein's, but the flavor of this story led me to include it here.

My wife and I met our neighbor while taking a walk on *Chol HaMoed Pesach* (the intervening days of Passover) six years ago (1986). We asked after the welfare of her relatives who remained in Russia. She said they were safe because they were too far away from Chernobyl to risk any contamination. Together, we commiserated about the fate of the three million Jews in Russia.

"Yes," she said, "they are suffering — but now, this *Pesach*, the communists will have to let the Jews go."

It was an astonishing remark. Her statement was shocking for two reasons. First, for the previous decade, Russian Jews were not allowed to emigrate. Secondly, what would motivate the communists to let the Jews go now?

"Why," I asked, "would the Russians have to let the Jews go?"

My neighbor responded cryptically, "We are too dangerous for them; they must let us go."

How could she say that? We were one of the weakest ethnic groups in Russia. We suffered greatly for being Jewish. Why would the Soviet empire perceive us as a threat?

She refused to answer the question directly and as we parted she said wistfully, "You will see. They will let us go now." She did not elaborate, yet she made this prediction with great certainty.

As soon as she said it, somehow we knew she had spoken the truth. But how to make sense of it? That night I tried to formulate an answer.

The disaster in Chernobyl produced the modern equivalent of the ten plagues and these plagues were "instantaneously" visited upon the Russian people. Unlike the Biblical Egyptians, the communists didn't have to wait for a sequence of plagues as they were embedded in the central meltdown.

First there were the afflictions of nature. The aquifers spread radiation through the Russian soil, contaminating the water supply and damaging the food chain. It was like the Nile, lifeline to all of Egypt, turning into blood thousands of years ago.

Furthermore, so complete was the devastation of nature that background music had to be piped in for the nuclear research teams because the total lack of any sound was driving the scientists crazy. The weather around Kiev began to change, similar to the Biblical pattern where fiery hailstorms assailed Egypt.

During the first weeks of the accident, the Minister of Defense denied that any disaster had occurred. He ordered the Russian army to stop citizens from leaving the area. In essence, he sentenced the inhabitants to the hidden death of radiation. In the profound 'darkness' of the communist system the natural feeling for their own Russian children was lost. They condemned their own first born.

Like Pharaoh, the Defense Minister's heart hardened as all the plagues afflicted Russia in turn. It was only a matter of time before the Jews had to be released. Deep down the Russians knew the score. God was bigger than the Kremlin.

As Rabbi Wein explains, "The Torah is more than a history book. It is not a subject to be taken in a 'Bible as Literature' class. If you have eyes to see and ears to hear, the Torah will reflect current events."

His congregant understood what really shapes the world. The celebration of the exodus from Egypt is recorded in *az yashir Moshe,* the song the Children of Israel sang at the Red Sea after they saw their adversaries drowned. The song has many parts, yet one central theme is clear: "He took us out with a strong hand and an outstretched arm," and He continues to do so.

Generation Gap

In his latest trip to Eretz Yisroel, Rabbi Wein attended morning services in a synagogue in Jerusalem. He relates that, unlike his own synagogue, which has benches facing the front of the synagogue, this synagogue had tables and benches, so he was forced to look at those praying opposite him. A tall, blue-eyed, blond-haired man and three blond small boys walked in and sat down opposite him. Rabbi Wein is used to the racial diversity of the citizens in Israel so little surprises him, but this was different; this particular family was definitely Aryan.

More noteworthy than their racial features was the seriousness and intensity of their praying. The children were especially well-behaved and followed the service dutifully without once wavering in their concentration. For Rabbi Wein, accustomed to the more freewheeling American child, it was an unusual experience.

Afterward, the Rabbi remarked to a friend that they looked like fine people. His friend said that the man was a microbiologist at Hebrew University who happened to have an extraordinary story to tell. "Would you like to hear it?" he asked, and without waiting for an answer, called to his fellow congregant, "Avraham, this is Rabbi Berel Wein. I'm sure he would like to hear your story."

The two shook hands and agreed to walk home together. As they went, the Rabbi listened to him tell the following story:

"I was born and brought up in Germany. My father was an officer in the elite Gestapo killing squad, the *Todtenkopf* (Deathhead Squad). He served throughout the war and after it was over successfully eluded apprehension. But his crimes were so heinous that years later the West German Republic continued to pursue him. Finally, he was caught and imprisoned for ten years. Later, because he was so old, they reduced his sentence and let him out after four and a half years. My father never talked about his past and when he was caught, I read about his crimes in the newspaper. It was a bewildering experience to find out that my father led such a monstrous life.

"The family was shaken by the news. I was a teenager and became very confused by all the notoriety. When we went to visit him in prison I couldn't go in to see him. I felt as if he betrayed me. However, one useful thing came out of this — I developed an interest in the War and found out as much as I could about the *Todtenkopf* and its role in the Holocaust.

"All this occurred around that time the Eichmann trial was taking place, and Holocaust material began to be published. I read all I could find and was able to get a general picture of what happened to the Jews. What I found out horrified me and the thought that my father took a role — a leading role in the slaughter — made me feel that perhaps our family was tainted with evil. If the conditions were the same, I asked myself, could I too become a killer?

"I took a trip getting as far away from Germany as possible. It was as if I was haunted by Germany and all things German. I remember that I didn't even want to read about Germany history. If Germany could do what it did in the Holocaust, then its past wasn't usable. It could give us nothing to live by in the future, and studying its history would do more harm than good.

"On the way, I decided to visit Israel to get some perspective on the victims of the Nazis and find out what was so special about this nation that so consumed Hitler. I needed to come to terms with what was churning inside of me and I toured the country, working periodically here and there on agricultural settlements.

"While in a kibbutz, I saw a poster advertising a summer's program at Hebrew University in desert zoology, and I enrolled. I did very well and in the fall was able to register for a graduate program at the University. While I was engaged in graduate work, I also became interested in Judaism.

"I loved Israel so much I just stayed on and applied for citizenship. Also, after about two years of learning about Judaism I decided to study to become a Jew. A few years later I earned my Ph.D. in microbiology and became a Jew. I married and settled in Jerusalem. My wife was a German Lutheran, but she, too, converted. A psychologist might interpret my conversion as sublimating my guilty feelings, but I prefer to think about it as fulfilling my Jewish destiny. Don't ask me how or why, but here we are — an observant Jewish family. And we are very happy living as Jews.

"About a year ago we learned that my father was not feeling well. My wife thought it would be a *mitzvah* to visit him and show him his grandchildren. At first I was apprehensive about going back to Germany, a country I now feared. But, in the end, I took a sabbatical and we went back to Darmstadt to visit with my father. It was quite a scene. My boys wore their *yarmulkas*, and had their *tzitzis* showing. Their *payos* (sidecurls) were tucked back behind their ears and, of course, they spoke Hebrew.

"When he first saw us, my father was overwhelmed, and, initially, couldn't bring himself to embrace anyone. Later we got to talk and he seemed to be pleased by the way things were turning out for us.

"My father is very old now, over ninety, and I wanted to know what he did to merit such a long life with such grandchildren, so I asked him point blank what he had done to earn his good fortune. I explained to him that we Jews believe that there are consequences to what we do and the reward system in life is measured very carefully. He looked at me and pondered the question.

"He answered, 'I can't think of anything outstanding but once, in Frankfurt,' he said, 'when we were rounding up the Jews, I had the chance to save the life of three Jewish boys who were hiding in a Catholic orphanage. For some reason they aroused my sympathy. I was touched by their plight; they were so lost and forlorn I felt pity for them, so I let them flee. I don't know what happened to them. But I didn't kill them.'

"I thought his answer over and told him that according to our tradition his answer made sense. 'You know, papa, if you had let four boys go, you would have had four grandchildren.' "

The Disco Rabbi

Rabbi Mayer Dovid Grossman, the spiritual leader of Migdal Ha'emek, visited Rabbi Wein and the Bais Torah congregation on a recent fundraising trip for his institution Migdal Ohr in the Galil. He told this story of his Rebbe, the Lelover Rebbe who had been admitted to a hospital for major surgery.

For the last twenty years, the Lelover Rebbe had been afflicted with a skin disease which covered most of his body. Besides being unsightly, the rash would produce an itch that was unbearable. However, as a younger man, the Rav had taken a vow that he would never touch his body below his waist. This type of vow has been regarded as a traditional spiritual exercise in self control and the Lelover took his vow very seriously.

With the help of God, for the last twenty years, he had succeeded in not overturning his oath. Now, however, he was very ill and the impending surgery required that he be given a general anaesthetic which would render him unconscious for several hours. This was the first time the Rebbe would be anaesthetized and he didn't know if upon awakening in a drugged state he would remember not to scratch his eczema. So great was his respect for making a *neder* (vow) that he felt he couldn't risk a violation. He asked Rabbi Grossman to assemble three distinguished Rabbis to make an effort to overturn his *neder*.

As Rabbi Grossman told the story, in his charmingly broken English, it was moving to hear how his Rebbe dealt with his spiritual crisis. Sometimes we learn a lot about a person as one describes the problems of others. To Rabbi Grossman, the crisis faced by his Rebbe was terrible. The purity of his whole world depended on not taking the Lord's name in vain. If this is the kind of model Rabbi Grossman values, then one can begin to understand the spiritual fires which burn within him.

Migdal Ohr (Rabbi Grossman's institution) specializes in people nobody else wants. These are people who were rejected by the rest of the world — convicts, dope addicts, the most troublesome kinds of social deviants. Rabbi Grossman, known throughout the world as the "Disco Rabbi," is famous for transforming these outcasts, an army of over 2,000 students, into productive, caring, observant Jews.

Rabbi Grossman earned the name "Disco Rabbi," because at the conclusion of Shabbos he used to visit the nightclubs in Tel Aviv and try to persuade young Israelis to become observant. Once he was working on such a fellow and asked the young man what it would take to get him to put on *tzitzis* and become Sabbath observant. The young man answered frankly: a Porsche convertible. The following Saturday night, the "Disco Rabbi" drove up to the nightclub in the sportscar and handed the keys to the youth. The youngster left the club, never to return again, and became a *baal teshuvah*.

Here was a man who put his money where his convictions were. To him, it was simply a spiritual transaction. "Is $30,000 too much to pay for a Jewish soul?" The incident instantly established Rabbi Grossman's reputation throughout Israel, and, along with the return of Israeli media star Uri Zohar, provided a great impetus for the Baal Teshuvah movement in Israel.

The scope of the success of Migdal Ohr makes one realize the enormous strength that can be released when one controls one's desires. Such is the power of good, refined Jews. They can transform the Galil through restraint alone.

Shomair Hatzair

Rabbi Wein told us this story after he got back from Israel. For some reason he tells the best stories while recovering from jet lag.

A young Jewish man, Mark, arrived in Israel with his Swedish girlfriend, whom he had befriended that summer in Paris. The couple registered with the main kibbutz organization as volunteer agricultural laborers. He stated he wanted a taste of the real Israel so they sent him into the Bet Sha'an valley to pick fruits on a Shomair Hatzair kibbutz (a kibbutz of ardent socialists). They forgot to tell him that in summer this kibbutz is the hottest place in the world.

When they signed in at the kibbutz main office the secretary, who was a real old-time bolshevik, assigned them to the guest house. They were given the task of harvesting bananas on the plantation.

After a few days on the job, Mark began to complain in the main office about his assignment. The heat was too much for him and he couldn't drink enough to stay ahead of its dehydrating effects. He hated working in such a climate because it drained him of all his energy. The secretary heard him out, then pulled Mark aside and told him confidentially, "This is no place for you. Go to a yeshiva in Jerusalem and they'll take care of you there." She gave him a slip with the name and address of the Ohr Somayach Yeshiva (a yeshiva in Jerusalem for interested latecomers to Judaism).

Mark protested halfheartedly, "What about my girlfriend?"

The secretary said that she would be taken care of in the kibbutz. "When you're ready to return, you'll see her if you want to." With that she gave him a bus ticket to Jerusalem. After saying good-bye to his friend and promising to return, Mark left.

The rabbis in Ohr Somayach took very good care of their kibbutz referral, and in a short while he became a *baal teshuvah* (a 'returnee' committed to Torah observance). Four years later he was traveling through the Bet Sha'an valley on the way to a yeshiva in Zichron Yaakov and decided to revisit the same kibbutz. Sure enough, the same secretary was at her desk dressed in the drab business-like outfit she wore originally. Mark, on the other hand, was dressed like a typical yeshiva man; black hat, black suit, white shirt and he had even managed to grow a very full, black beard.

"Are you sure you're in the right office?" she asked. From the way she looked at him, he knew she didn't remember their past encounter. He refreshed her memory and when she recalled him, he asked her why she had sent him away from the kibbutz into the arms of the "enemy."

She replied that she knew instantly that the socialist ideal was not for Mark. "I could tell from your eyes, that kibbutz life was not for you. You needed something else. So I sent you ahead. I wasn't wrong, was I?"

Israelis are different from Americans — they look you straight in the eyes when they talk to you, and some will even tell you what they see.

Yossel the Mohel

In the Sephardi synagogue in Bayit Vegan in Jerusalem, the new father recited the blessings for his son's *bris milah*. Yossel, the famous Jerusalem *mohel*, was performing the circumcision. This old-time Yerushalmi, a veteran of thousands of circumcisions, listened to the father's impassioned recitation of the blessings. He recited it clearly, emphasizing every syllable. As he focused on his holy work, Yossel noted the extra serious rendition of the blessing and said simply to the *sandek* (godfather), who was holding the baby on a pillow on his lap, "He must be a *baal teshuvah*."

The *sandek* agreed ."I know, I'm the grandfather and this is my first *bris* as a *sandek*. Can you make it fast? I'm not feeling too good."

The Mexican-American Traffic Cop

Rabbi Wein was invited to serve as a scholar-in-residence for a Spring weekend in a synagogue in Southern California. In this synagogue, many of the members were professional people. Everyone had graduate degrees. The *gabbai* was a computer engineer with degrees from MIT and University of Chicago. His wife graduated from Berkeley and had a Masters from Stanford in public health administration.

During the *Shabbos* services, the *gabbai* called out the honors of holding up and then dressing the Torah in its vestments. The expressions used are *"Ya'amod haMagbiah"* (the one who is to raise the Torah come forth) and *"Ya'amod haGolal"* (the one who is to dress the Torah come forth). The *gabbai* thought he has enunciated it very clearly, but when Rabbi Wein heard it, it came out *"Ya'amod hava negillah."*

The engineer explained that he got his job as *gabbai* by default, because most of the other members spoke even less Hebrew than he. When Rabbi Wein asked him why he became a *baal teshuvah*, he explained it was all due to a traffic jam and a Mexican-American cop.

"I was a hotshot engineer, and was late for an appointment with a vendor who was supplying my company with electronic equipment. I drove down the main street of this town in the valley and got caught in traffic. It was late on a Sunday afternoon in September, an unusual time of day for there to be such a jam. I couldn't understand what was causing it until I spotted a Mexican-American police officer holding up the cars to allow a large group of well-dressed people cross the avenue. Impatiently, I sounded my horn. Immediately, this big, mustachioed, traffic cop walked over to my car and accused me of being a little quick on the horn.

" 'I'm trying to get to my business appointment,' I said in defense.

" 'Well, these people are trying to get some place too. These are Jewish people and tonight is their holy day, Yom Kippur. That building over there is their synagogue.' He pointed to a fairly large modern structure across the street. It had a Jewish star over the main entrance. 'Why don't you just cool it for a while?'

"I was so embarrassed by my impatience and ignorance that I vowed right then and there to start learning about my religion. Imagine, a Mexican-American traffic cop knew when *Yom Kippur* was, and I didn't!"

Talmid Kokom

One of the Rabbis in Shaarei Torah told this story in the teachers' room of the Yeshiva. Not all the stories at Shaarei Torah originate with the Dean.

There is a middle-aged man in Lakewood, New Jersey who is one of the most diligent learners there. He has an unconventional background. He served as a Marine during the Vietnam War and was wounded during one of the campaigns in the central highlands after the Tet Offensive. Although his physical injuries were extensive, the major damage done to him was psychological. To this day he will not speak of his experiences just before he was wounded.

As part of his program of rehabilitation he was sent to a Naval Veterans Hospital in the middle of New Jersey. While he was recovering from his wounds he expressed a desire to learn about his religious heritage and permission was granted to visit the Lakewood Yeshiva. He became interested in learning about Torah and requested that during his recuperation he be granted leave to learn full-time at the Yeshiva.

His request was granted. In a short period of time he became a *baal teshuvah* and started a life as a serious student of Jewish traditions.

While at Lakewood, the Navy granted him full disability pay. Periodically, however, the Veterans Administration would review his record to determine his continuing eligibility. After three years, a medical examination team decided that he was fully recovered and recommended his allowance be terminated. The ex-marine appealed this decision and a special tribunal of three naval commanders was chosen to review the case.

The Navy argued that this veteran was functioning on a high level. Every one admitted he had made a full recovery intellectually, but the Naval doctors also felt he was ready to adjust to the pressures of the workaday world.

In his defense, the yeshiva student claimed that, for the present, he had only one vocational goal: to be a Torah scholar. Eventually he would leave Lakewood and become a teacher, but right now it would be unfair to deprive him of his financial support. He feared what would happen to him if he were forced to leave learning.

"Why should we subsidize what is essentially a religious vocation?" the panel queried. "We are only sanctioned to support real vocations or professional occupations. We cannot break the law and support religious vocation. Rabbinical preparation is not an approved course of study."

The student countered, "I want to become a *'talmid chochum.'* In rabbinical programs, one can learn to become a Rabbi. But I don't want to do that. I want to become a *talmid chochum*."

The panel wanted to know the meaning of the term. The student answered: "A *talmid chochum* is a learned person who knows right from wrong and who can help others make ethical decisions. Many of our great Jewish leaders never became Rabbis. A *talmid chochum* has no synagogue and no real job. His work is only to learn the Torah. I know enough now to become a Rabbi, but I still feel I have to learn more to become a *talmid chochum*. If you cut my disability pay you will force me out of my pattern of education. I might even lose the learning I've already acquired."

One of the Naval panelists, a former commander, said he knew what the ex-marine was talking about. He had seen *talmid 'kokums'* in action. (The commander pronounced *chochum* with a hard 'k' sound because there is no equivalent sound in English.) "They read from those long books, don't they, these *talmid 'kokums'*?"

"Yes, they do. The books are called the Talmud," answered the yeshiva man.

The naval commander informed the other officers that when he commanded a destroyer in the China Sea during the Korean War, a Jewish Chaplain on board asked permission to learn the Talmud with two Jewish sailors. He, too, was a *talmid 'kokum'* and needed to learn Talmud on a regular basis.

"We were at sea off the coast of China during the Korean War for three straight months. When we hit port in Japan for a little rest and recuperation, it was a wild scene. Even before we docked, fights broke out on deck to see who would be the first off the ship. Discipline was breaking down in front of my eyes. Well, there were these two Jewish sailors and the chaplain who were learning their Talmud on the port main deck just off the sailors' quarters. Even amidst the wild behavior they went about their learning. I don't know what they were learning, but the commotion of the sailors getting ready for liberty didn't affect them at all. It seemed as if they were used to studying in such a clamorous atmosphere.

"It turned out their quiet scholarliness affected the others. My men couldn't help but notice that the *talmid 'kokums'* were studying and not behaving like madmen. Their learning made an impression on the rest of the crew. They settled down because of this. At least they left the ship in one piece. Coming back to ship was a different story.

"I'd like to make a recommendation that we grant this man another year of full compensation. Being a *talmid 'kokum'* is serious business. These people just want to learn. Call it occupational therapy, if you will."

The commander's recommendation carried the day, and the appeals panel extended his benefits for another year.

> *Five years later, the Vietnam talmid 'kokum' is still in Lakewood. We don't know if his benefits are extended, but he is still involved in 'occupational therapy' and rumor has it that he has even become a big talmid kokum.*

A Baal Teshuvah Story

Slowly, Jesse Goldwurm trudged up from the pond where he had caught a small "St. Peter's fish." Reputed to be tasty, it was a challenge to eat because of the many small bones. Jesse knew enough about the area to appreciate his good luck. "Probably no one catches anything edible up here," he thought. He was five kilometers into the mountains of the Sinai, north of Eilat.

On this trip, fishing was not his prime concern, though. He was here because he needed time to decide what to do with his life. Under a sandstone outcropping he gathered a few dried leaves and twigs, set up a crude grill, and cooked the fish. As the fish fried in the oil, he reflected on his recent stay in the Jewish Quarter in Jerusalem.

A few short weeks ago, in the Old City, Rabbi Shuster had introduced himself to Jesse and invited him for a *Shabbos* dinner at a nearby yeshiva called Aish HaTorah. One thing led to another and before he knew it a soft-spoken young Rabbi was teaching Jesse the "Sayings of Our Fathers." He found it to be a rich intellectual experience.

Aish HaTorah is what is called a *Baal Teshuvah* Yeshiva, a place where Jews motivated to return to their spiritual source can learn. After three weeks at the yeshiva, he contemplated taking a leave of absence from his graduate studies in America and studying full time at 'Aish.' But he wasn't sure he was ready. So he took a week and went to the mountains around Eilat to delve into himself. Did he have enough commitment to be that Jewish?

He ate his meal with some Maccabee Beer he had brought in his backpack. When he'd finished, he took out his pocket-sized English *siddur* and tried to figure out the appropriate after-blessing. He found no blessing for fish so he just said the general blessing, *borei nefashos*.

Later on he would recall the fish smelled a little peculiar, but at the time he ignored the warning. He didn't want to spoil his good time. He surveyed the mountain setting, his open-air dining room. In the stony rubble before him, he noticed large rocks arrayed like chairs on a dusty lawn. He sat back under the outcropping and took it all in. Using the cliff wall as backing, he dozed off.

It was still light when he awoke with pains in his stomach. They were sharp stabbing pains unlike anything he had ever experienced. Gasping for air, his felt his throat parched dry. There was one can of beer left in his pack, but it was too far for him to reach. So bad was his stomach seizure, he could hardly move. "It must have been the fish," he thought. He was certain it was poisonous.

Deeply alarmed, he called out past the rocks. "Help me!" There was no response, not even an echo. His stomach was cramping sharply and he wished he could retch up what he had eaten, but he was too desiccated to rid himself of the poisonous fish. He called out again, but this time, to his horror, could manage no more than a hoarse whisper. His throat was now dangerously dry. He doubled over in the dust, fearing the worst.

The next thing he saw was a big brown toe. It belonged to a tall, robed figure who appeared out of nowhere and now towered over Jesse. In slow motion, a bearded, brown face lowered itself to the ground. Face to face now, this strange apparition offered him help.

In flawless English, Jesse heard the brown man's words: "Hello there, can I help you? I'm a doctor." The words were gently spoken. Jesse shook his head affirmatively. He couldn't believe his eyes.

He must be hallucinating. What was this man doing masquerading in the Sinai as a doctor? He straightened up as best he could and tried to focus on the apparition standing above him. A tall, slim, white-bearded black man, about fifty, came into view. The man wore a spotless white robe and old sandals.

He crouched, his head barely three feet from Jesse's face. Jesse remembered that his first impression was positive. The man sounded sincere, spoke clearly, and Jesse sensed that he was a refined man. Still, the central question remained: What was a black doctor doing in the middle of the Sinai Desert?

"I ate some bad fish, I think, and unless I get out of here I am going to die from stomach cramps."

As he stooped over to examine him, the black man leaned forward very close to Jesse, almost face to face. Jesse slumped as the "doctor's" hands reached down and began to knead his stomach and abdomen.

After about a minute the "doctor" concluded, "You don't have appendicitis, thank God. You were right, you have been poisoned. If we can get some apple juice into you, you will recover. There's a small kibbutz on the other side of the mountain. I'll walk around to it and be back in half an hour with something that will help you. Don't drink the beer you have in your knapsack; I'll just wet your face with it."

As the man wet him with a few drops of beer, Jesse mustered some strength and said weakly, "Thank you — I don't even know your name."

"Rafael."

Suddenly, the black man stood up and leaped deftly onto a small boulder.

"My friend, before I help you further," he said, "I must know something." Jesse didn't know what was coming next. The pause seemed to last an eternity.

"Are you Jewish?" the black man asked, folding his arms and waiting for a reply.

The question caught Jesse completely off guard and was worrisome. The man could be a P.L.O. terrorist, or part of the "Black Hebrews," a strange sect of Afro-Americans who migrated to Israel. Who knew what he wanted.

Jesse did not know what to do, but then he thought about the lessons about Jewish pride he had been taught at Aish HaTorah. "I'm Jewish," he declared almost belligerently. "Of course, I'm Jewish." He had suddenly found his voice and spoke clearly. And as he uttered the words, surprisingly, he noted the pain began to subside.

"I'm glad you're Jewish," said the white-robed figure who smiled and, leaping from stone to stone, disappeared behind the mountain. In a twinkling, Jesse was left alone.

In time, the black man reappeared carrying a blue thermos bottle filled with apple juice. He fed the juice to Jesse and mumbled some Hebrew words in a melodious chant. Within ten minutes Jesse's pains departed and he started to breathe normally. The crisis had passed.

"Would it have made a difference if I weren't Jewish?" asked Jesse.

The stranger didn't answer the question. Instead he said, "I have to go now. Someone at the kibbutz needs my attention. I'll see you there later tonight. You'll be recovered by then." And he disappeared as suddenly as he had come.

In a couple of hours, Jesse arose, his health restored. He hiked slowly around the mountain and found a small date plantation about a half mile away at the bottom of a hill. He asked several people if they knew of a black doctor, Rafael, who had borrowed apple juice from them. One kibbutznik laughed out loud. "Rafael, *malach shel cholim? Lo Po.*" ("Rafael, angel of the sick? He is not here.")

Jesse did not understand the reference to Rafael the Angel. (According to Jewish tradition, Rafael is the angel in charge of curing sick people.) The kibbutzniks had never seen a black man in their village, and no one had borrowed apple juice from them. They visited Eilat when they needed medical attention. "You suffered a heat stroke," they said to him consolingly. "Hallucinations are common."

Jesse was confused. Could it really have been an hallucination? He mulled over the possibility as he thanked the villagers for their assistance and asked for directions to Eilat. One of them offered to take him in his truck. As he picked up his knapsack to depart, suddenly Jesse noticed something — the blue thermos.

A chill shot down his spine. He turned to one of the kibbutzniks and said, "Please return this thermos to Dr. Rafael when he does show up." Jesse then handed the bottle to one of them and concluded, "I didn't have a chance to rinse it out."

The kibbutznik uncapped the thermos and held it up to his nose suspiciously. He smelled the faint sweetness of apple juice and passed it around to the others for confirmation. No one spoke until he left.

Jesse returned to Eilat and bought a ticket back to Jerusalem on the first bus.

> *Jesse is married now, has four children and lives in Bnei Brak. He told this story at the Shabbos table of Rabbi Hertzel Shechter, an administrator of Yeshiva Aish HaTorah. Rabbi Shechter lives in the Neve Yaakov neighborhood in Jerusalem.*
>
> *After Rabbi Shechter told this story at a fundraiser in Bais Torah, Rabbi Wein added the following words: "God has seen fit to revive the Jewish people with large infusions of idealism and energy. In this hedonistic period of time, when most young people are absorbed in pursuing careers and wealth, the Baal Teshuvah Movement has risen. It has attracted, against all odds, the most talented young Jews who have dedicated themselves to a Torah way of life. This powerful movement is further evidence that the Jewish people are immortal and that God will not*

abandon them, or allow them to drift aimlessly and mindlessly through the barren wasteland of contemporary society."

5

The Song of a Yeshiva

The philosophical question most heard in American Yeshiva high schools is: "Is Bazooka bubble gum kosher or not?"

We think heaven is a boring place. Rav Aaron Kotler gave a charitable man a blessing that in the World to Come he would sit and study Torah all day, every day, forever. The man frowned. Rav Kotler said, "Don't worry, the blessing is that you'll want to do it."

The Song of a Yeshiva

ing Solomon says in the Song of Songs: "Many waters cannot extinguish the fire of this love; nor rivers wash it away. Were any man to offer all the treasure of his home to entice you away from your love, they would scorn you to the extreme."

The Sages tell a story in regard to this verse. The great Rabbi Yochanan, who was already quite old, was walking from Tiberias to Safed, in the north of Israel. It's only a distance of 18 miles, but it's a strenuous and circuitous uphill climb. Rabbi Yochanan was poor and could not afford a donkey. His students were accompanying him, and when they passed a certain field Rabbi Yochanan said, "This field once belonged to me, but I sold it for the sake of the yeshiva."

Later, they passed an orchard and again Rabbi Yochanan remarked, "That orchard once belonged to me, but I sold it in order to maintain the yeshiva." And once again, while passing a luxuriant vineyard, Rabbi Yochanan paused to say, "That vineyard too once was mine, but I sold it for the sake of the yeshiva."

His disciples wept when they considered their master's condition: "Woe to us that we must see you this way. You once had so much, and now you are old, tired, broken, and you have to go on foot." But Rabbi Yochanan replied, "You should rejoice to see me this way. I do not have one moment's regret."

The love that Rabbi Yochanan had for Torah, for his students, for eternity — "Many waters cannot extinguish the fire of this love."

Rabbi Wein often uses this story to describe the essence of a yeshiva: "When I hear the boys in our yeshiva learning, and one calls out melodically, 'Rabbi Yochanan said this . . . ' and another responds, 'Rabbi Yochanan said that . . .,'I get excited. Rabbi Yochanan has not been with us for almost 1,800 years. Does anyone remember anything about Rabbi Yochanan's fields? Or the fields of the biggest landowners of that time? Or who was the richest Jew alive at that time? No one knows! It has all been swallowed up and covered by the sands of time.

"But today — right now — you can still hear Jewish children pronouncing the name of Rabbi Yochanan. He is still here. His Torah is still here. 'Many waters cannot extinguish the fire of his love.' "

Boys Town

When Rabbi Wein was in Israel several years ago, he received a call from an old, good friend, Rabbi Alexander Sender Linchner. Rabbi Linchner is the director of Boys Town in Jerusalem, a school that caters to the educational and religious needs of thousands of young men in Israel. The institution prepares them to be anything from rabbis to electricians — or both — *Chanoch l'naar al pi darko*. ("Teach the young man according to his way.")

Rabbi Linchner was eager to give the Rabbi the grand tour: "I'm leaving a wake-up call for 6:00 A.M. and I'll be in the lobby of your hotel to pick you up at 6:25." Rabbi Wein had just flown into Israel and would have preferred the afternoon showing, but he acquiesced.

They arrived in time for the 6:45 morning *minyan* in the main study hall. There are several *minyanim* every morning in Boys Town, the melting pot of Torah education, to serve the diverse customs of its students — Ashkenazi, Sephardi, Taimani, Russian and Ethiopian. Each group was provided the opportunity to worship God in the way it could express itself best.

Rabbi Wein was interested: "After an Ashkenazi service, Rabbi Linchner showed me the other *minyanim*, which were finishing up. You would not have noticed much difference in the *minyanim*, the concentration of all participants was so intense. If I could bring my synagogue on Yom Kippur to the level of devotion I witnessed there on a weekday I would feel I have accomplished something as a Rav.

"Rabbi Linchner introduced me to a twenty-year-old Ethiopian lad who had come to the Holy Land during Operation Moses the previous year. In nine months, the young man had almost caught up with the 2,500 years that separated his hometown from the modern state of Israel. He could learn a page of Talmud, spoke a fluent Hebrew, and was learning computer programing.

"We sat down to breakfast in the main dining room and I asked him if it was the first time he had seen a plane when the Israelis airlifted him over from Ethiopia.

" 'Forget the plane,' he said. 'It was the first time we had seen stairs!' "

❦ ❦ ❦

One of the newly arrived Russian students, a sixteen year old who didn't know how to read Hebrew, and certainly not Aramaic when he arrived in Boys Town two years ago, took to learning as if he was born to it — which, in a way, he was (every Jew is given the Torah as his inheritance). He learned the *Gemara Bava Kama,* a volume of the Talmud which deals with the laws of civil damages, and was able to recite the first nine chapters by heart. For him, it was not such an extraordinary accomplishment. "After all," he explained, "After we learn how to operate a computer we learn *gemara* for six hours every day. What else can we do but learn it thoroughly?"

> And so the kibbutz golius (ingathering of the exiles) continues apace as the Lord assembles talent from countries that don't have stairs, and recruits teenagers who learn the laws of Talmud and the laws of computers for seventy hours a week.

Rabbi Mendel Kaplan

One of the most colorful rabbis ever to arrive on the shores of Lake Michigan was Rabbi Mendel Kaplan, a Rebbe at what is today the Skokie Yeshiva. He was a strong personality who didn't let temporary inconveniences interfere with the way things had to go — his way. Because of his vast knowledge of Torah and familiarity with the ways of world, he was able to make the Talmud seem real to his students.

His first day in America was spent teaching Talmud to thirty fourteen-year-old American boys. Europe did not produce that special young adult we call the American teenager and Rabbi Kaplan was having a rough time. To complicate matters he knew no English and his students knew little Yiddish. The boys did not know the Rabbi had just arrived that morning from Europe. For his part, he didn't know that "Chicago was the hog butcher of the world," nor did he know precious else about America and her folkways. He thought the National League was the successor to the League of Nations. To put it mildly, he was in the dark.

That first day, the level of classroom communication was low. He didn't know the names of his students and, to the boys' delight, didn't even know what an attendance book was designed to do. Due to the language difficulty, when they recited from the Talmud, his explanations and corrections were incomprehensible. Needless to say, that first day was long and stressful.

When they went home, many of the boys revealed to their parents that they didn't think Rabbi Kaplan would last too long. The next day the boys came to class expecting more of the same, but they were very surprised when Rabbi Kaplan marched in with a copy of the daily newspaper, *The Chicago Tribune*. He opened the paper and told the boys, "Today, you are going to teach me English and I am going to teach you how to read a newspaper."

After the class recovered from its disbelief, they settled into what must have been one of the most unusual Torah lessons of all time.

The boys would read the news stories slowly in English while Reb Mendel followed along as best he could, index finger always "on the place." The boys who knew a little Yiddish would translate haltingly. At the conclusion of each piece Rabbi Kaplan would interpret the events from a Jewish point of view as only a canny Torah master could. The effect was thrilling. By the end of the day he had learned over fifty American idioms and a fair amount of grammar and they had learned that philosophic and Talmudic themes underlie all current events. Unlike *The Jewish Daily*

Forward, which printed stories about everyday Jewish life in America, the gentile newspapers, as analyzed by Rav Kaplan, dealt with classical Jewish themes.

For example, he compared the economic boom that America was undergoing in the post-war years with a story from the Talmud: King David was beset by a desperate need of money. His minister told him to "go out as a band of warriors." And so it was, military expansion stimulated the economy and filled the king's treasure house.

Even entertainment and fashions could be delineated from a Jewish perspective. No one quite remembers how he dealt with the sports world. But in the era before Kaplan's arrival Hank Greenberg, the Jewish slugger from Detroit, had hit 58 homers one season. The boys, ever starved for an authentic Jewish sports hero, idolized "Hank" and asked the Rabbi if Greenberg could ever break Babe Ruth's record.

The Rabbi didn't know a baseball from a knish, but he knew that in a gentile world it's best to keep a low profile. He told his boys not to place too much hope on Jews who compete in the gentile world. "Sports is for Americans; Greenberg is not an American name. Mr. Henry Greenberg will not replace the 'Baby' no matter what he does." These were the years when Greenberg was not named to the All-Star team because his name was not Gehrig or McGowan; Reb Mendel had understood the game even though he didn't know the rules.

In the eyes of the American boys, this European Rabbi was someone from whom you could learn. By the end of the second day, after Reb Mendel had finished *The Tribune,* victory was his. He had wiped out the memory of the first disastrous day and the boys were now on his side.

And so it went for the rest of his first year in the Chicago Yeshiva. Reb Mendel brought in the daily edition of *The Chicago Tribune,* and after class he learned English from the stories the boys read to him. By the end of the semester he had learned to speak English and his students began to learn that their Talmud was much more than an ancient text.

❦ ❦ ❦

When the boys returned to their learning, Reb Mendel continued to read in class. He had the extraordinary knack of doing two things at the same time. Even though he was reading or attending to something quite different from the discussion at hand, he knew exactly where the boys were holding in their analyses of *Rashi* and *Tosafos*. He was an omnivorous reader and would begin to read anything and everything. One day there was a book on his desk that not only perpetuated the nonsense of a "second" Isaiah, but actually had an illustration of him! His students were riveted to see his reaction. He calmly picked up the book and threw it across the room in a perfect arc directly into the wastebasket. The boys appreciated his idiosyncrasies; he was a very different kind of man who made the long Yeshiva day seem much shorter than it was.

A legend in his own time, Rabbi Kaplan was fond of repeating the idea of the Sages that students would really understand their mentors only after forty years had gone by; it held true in Rabbi Kaplan's case as well. Only after a long period of maturation did the men who learned with him as boys appreciate the insights of that powerful mind.

Rabbi Kaplan Shorts

Rabbi Kaplan used to say, "Be careful what you pray for; you might actually get it."

The best marital counseling also came from Rabbi Kaplan. He gave it to all his students in Philadelphia who were preparing for marriage: *"Men darf avekgeben a bissel selfishness."* ("One has to give up a little selfishness.")

Non-Conformists

The following is taken from Rabbi Wein's Jewish history tape series, tape 45, The Dawn of the Seventeenth Century. After introducing the character of Boruch Spinoza, the brilliant philosopher who was eventually excommunicated from the Jewish community because of his pantheistic ideas, Rabbi Wein goes off on a tangent concerning 'anti-establishment' personalities.

"Anti-establishment people make us uncomfortable. We like people who conform. The truth is, however, that many of the great Jews were not always the easiest students. Rabbi Yaakov Kaminetzky, zt'l, told me once that Rabbi Chaim Ozer Grodzensky, the Rav of Vilna until the Second World War, and, in our century, the pillar of Eastern European Jewry — a man of brilliance, erudition and piety — said that when he was twelve years old, his Rebbe threw him out of yeshiva because he brought a goat to the class one day. He said the goat knew how to learn as well as the Rebbe, and he brought it into class to emphasize the point. The Rebbe promptly gave him the boot.

"I can't prove it," Rabbi Weins continues, "but I have a sneaking suspicion that a lot of the great Jewish people got kicked out of school. It's not written in their biographies, but life is not always an ArtScroll biography.

"As an aside, I have a friend in Israel whose example gives me strength. Once, he went and stood in line all night to buy World Series tickets, which he promptly scalped the next day for three or four times the price. However, unbeknownst to him, the man he sold them to was an undercover policeman for the Chicago Police Department. They took him, this yeshiva kid of thirteen or fourteen, and put him in jail for the night so he should remember the lesson.

"The next day it was all over the papers: 'Yeshiva student scalps tickets.' The yeshiva was in an uproar. Back in our day, it was as if you would have taken a machine gun and mowed down seventy innocent people in the street. He was a marked man! How was the administration going to react? Would they take him back in the yeshiva or not?

"Luckily, we had a clever dean, Rabbi Greenberg. I happened to be near the office when he told the others his answer. One of the rabbis came up to him and said, 'You know, we have to kick this kid out. He made a *chilul Hashem* (desecration of God's name). It's all over the newspapers: yeshiva student in jail for scalping World Series tickets.'

"Without missing a beat, Rabbi Greenberg answered: 'I looked through the entire *Shulchan Aruch* (Code of Jewish Law) and didn't find the Chicago Cubs anywhere.'

That was his comment. He played down the entire incident.

"My friend eventually graduated and became a leading congregant in Chicago. He lives in Israel now, learns regularly, and has merited to have marvelous children and grandchildren. If they would have thrown him out of the yeshiva, what would have happened to him? He was lucky that he had Greenberg on his side. (Not Hank. Hank Greenberg was on the other team, Detroit.)"

In the Beginning

The Talmud relates, *Kol hascholos kashos*, ("All beginnings are difficult.") And for Rabbi Wein, things were no different. His yeshiva career got off to a dismal start. He now recalls his first day in the Chicago Yeshiva (now the Skokie Yeshiva) with good humor and the pleasure of knowing that even in the worst of times there is always a lesson to be learned.

At the age of eleven Rabbi Wein began attending a formal yeshiva. Until then he had been accustomed to coming home from public school at 3:00 P.M. and learning with his father, Rav Zev Wein, for three hours until suppertime. Because Rabbi Wein was very advanced for his years, when he entered the high school he was thrust into a Talmud class of fourteen-year-olds.

Because he was so small they sat him at the head of the class — squarely in front of the teacher. Young Berel Wein was very intimidated by the three-year age gap between him and his classmates and throughout that first day's class, his stomach was playing games with the small breakfast he had managed to force down that morning. The problem become more and more unmanageable and as the Rebbe read the first *Tosafos* of the year, Berel Wein did what any youngster would do in the same situation — he threw up.

The humiliation was indescribable. The Rebbe cleaned it up while the rest of the class whispered to one another. Afterward, the Rebbe called his newest student over to his desk and reassured him. "I don't want you to feel badly, so I will share with you the story of my first day in yeshiva." The Rebbe proceeded to tell him about his own yeshiva days in Kelm.

The Kelm Yeshiva had a very strong *mussar* (ethical improvement emphasis) flavor to it as well as a touch of Prussian discipline. The story is told that when the yeshiva was forced into exile during the First World War, the building attendant would walk into the empty study of the empty school, give a bang on the table and announce, *"Ershta seder"* (first session of the day). Such was the discipline of the yeshiva.

"I was also eleven years old when I got there," the Rebbe reminisced. "I remember that on my first *Shabbos* there, the yeshiva head, Rav Eliyahu Lopian, gave a talk about *gehinnom* (Hell) and I was scared silly."

("We are not afraid of *gehinnom* today," Rabbi Wein says. "We feel we've been there and back, so it's not real to us. But to them it was a very real place — it was palpable reality.")

"That first week," the Rebbe continued, "the *mashgiach* (rebbe in charge of the boys' spiritual well-being) came over to me just as I walked into the building and invited me to his office for a small chat. Like any good *mashgiach,* he wanted to have a personal relationship with each boy. But before we talked, he told me, 'Why don't you take off your coat?' So, without thinking, I just dumped my coat on the nearest chair. Noticing how I treated my coat, the *mashgiach* said, 'Oy, if that's the way it looks on the outside, imagine what it must be on the inside.' That's the internal turmoil of a young boy in strange surroundings. So, don't feel bad."

> *It was the Rebbe's sensitivity to the feelings of his student that allowed Berel Wein to put his first experience behind him and develop into a productive member of the yeshiva.*

Essay Contest

> *"I think the most painful experience a young person can have is to feel that what he is doing is meaningless — that it does not make a difference — and has no real value." — Rabbi Wein*

Not long ago, the yeshiva conducted a contest that required writing a research paper on a certain topic. Rules were posted on the bulletin board stating, among other things, when the paper had to be handed in. And then, two days after the deadline, a boy walked in and handed his paper to Rabbi Wein. Rabbi Wein took it and said, "I'm very appreciative of the fact that you did the work, but I also cannot count the paper toward the prize."

"Why can't you count it?"

Rabbi Wein answered that it was supposed to be in two days earlier. "It said in the bulletin, by 12:30 P.M."

"But I didn't read that line. I didn't know anything about it," the boy countered petulantly.

The Rabbi reminded him of the rules, "Look, the rules are the rules."

The boy just had a fit. Then he looked at the Rabbi and said, "So you mean I did it for nothing?" To which Rabbi Wein replied, "No, you didn't do it for nothing. You should never feel that you did something for nothing. There is nothing in the world that is done for nothing. You're just not in the running for the prize, but that doesn't mean that your work is for nothing. I'll read the paper and I'll grade it. I'll go over the paper with you; you'll have a benefit from it and I'll have a benefit from it."

Later, in a speech before a local education group, Rabbi Wein used the incident to make the following observations: "But he, being only fifteen years old, and having been raised in this country (where the eyes are on the prize), still felt that he did it for nothing. Since it didn't count in the contest, he felt it had no value.

"Our Sages, in Jewish tradition, saw that the problems of life are meaningful. God is not just putting us through an obstacle course simply to amuse Himself. Rather, every problem that occurs in a person's life — from the smallest to the largest — has a purpose and fits into a pattern. If a person would realize that it all fits a meaningful design, then failure and suffering could be turned into something advantageous; and pain itself would, necessarily, not be meaningless."

Yeshiva Lunchrooms

When Rabbi Wein went to yeshiva in Chicago, the lunches were not culinary triumphs. In those days, yeshivas were on hard times, and couldn't afford more than basic nourishment, but the boys didn't know this. They thought it was the cook's fault. Every day they went for lunch, she served red jello and yellow egg salad. One month, they even made a count: thirteen days in a row, they had red jello and yellow egg salad. They didn't know that someone had donated the eggs and the school got a good buy on the jello.

So the boys (all of them about fourteen years old) called a meeting to complain formally. They signed a petition and submitted it to the administrators, in effect demanding some variety in the menu. (Rabbi Wein recalls that one of the students, who is now Dean of a yeshiva in Israel, proposed that they have red egg salad and yellow jello — at least they would have variety!)

They submitted the petition saying that the lunch menu was not conducive to learning. It wasn't right, they wrote, "We learn all day and we need a better choice of food. If the *talmidim*, (students) don't deserve it, then change the food out of respect for the Talmud."

The cook found out about it and, the next day, she didn't show up for work. "To tell you the truth," Rabbi Wein recalls, "we didn't know she was gone. But for three or four days she didn't show. She got wind of the petition and was deeply hurt because you can't criticize the food without criticizing the cook.

"There's a lesson in jello," he observes. "It's the same lesson in the Talmud: don't embarrass your friend in public. If you're going to complain about the food, you're criticizing the cook and there are ramifications to criticizing the cook. For thirty or thirty-five years Reb Chaim of Volozhin ate food his wife prepared which he didn't like. He ate the food without saying a word. Why didn't he complain? Because there are ramifications to criticizing the cook."

Rabbi Wein concludes, "There's a balance here. You don't hire a cook who is inept, but there are things that have to taken into account."

The lunch menu at Rabbi Wein's yeshiva, Shaarei Torah, avoids the charge of dullness of menu — it always has a choice of two main dishes, sports a salad bar and even offers some kosher creole cooking. The food happens to be very tasty and few complaints are registered, at least not with the cook — he is six-foot-four and doesn't suffer fools lightly .

❧ ❧ ❧

Editor's note: In the Yeshiva I went to, we had kasha varnishkes Sunday, Monday, Wednesday and Friday and spaghetti with tomato sauce on Tuesday and Thursday. By the time I graduated, eight years later, the walls of the lunchroom reeked from the pungent smell of kasha. "Groats" — the word itself made me gag. After I got married, the first home cooked meal my wife made for me was kasha varnishkes. I wish I had heard the rabbi's speech above before I got married; it would have saved much unpleasantness.

❧ ❧ ❧

Probably the most popular person on the Shaarei Torah campus is the assistant cook. He is a very large human being who rarely smiles at the students but whom they all respect anyway. He is fair, exceedingly honest, and a firm disciplinarian who also knows how to prepare institutional food and make it taste home cooked. He is the anchor of decorum in a lunchroom that can turn hectic when it doubles as a basketball arena.

He has been known to adjudicate disputes with one arm while stirring the cocoa with the other. For many years he lived alone. Now, since the revolution in his country, Haiti, he has been reunited with his family and appears to be a lot happier, even smiling now and then.

His mysterious demeanor is an excellent cover for his warm personality. He never displays anger toward anyone. The students are respectful, yet are not afraid to approach him. Rabbi Wein says about him, "If he could learn a *blatt Gemara* (page of Talmud) with *Rashi* and *Tosafos,* I would make him dean, his *midos* (character traits) are so outstanding."

Snow Days

On the Shaarei Torah bulletin board located prominently in the main hallway are posted the rules and regulations covering the school calendar for the full year. The paragraph covering school closings due to snow and cold weather is a reprint of the regulations written by the Superintendent of Schools for the Fairbanks, Alaska school system:

". . . Schools will be closed only after six hours of -32 Fahrenheit, and if there are at least two feet of snowfall."

Ever since the regulations were posted seven years ago, the Monsey area has been spared any severe winters or snowfall substantial enough to close the school. This year the sign has been taken down. We await developments.

Abraham Lincoln's Drawer

"As Dean of a modern American yeshiva, I wear a black hat and so do my rabbis. Some of my students wear other kinds of hats and some even attempt to wear sneakers. We are usually successful in changing these students' footwear but initially we pretend we don't see the sneakers. We also pretend we don't hear their language. Every teacher has to act as if he's deaf and blind at times; sometimes even dumb. Through this pretense, we help them grow out of their adolescence.

"This year, one of the yeshiva students was acting up in class. His rabbi complained that he had never seen such a contemptuous young man before. Rejecting authority, the boy refused to do any of the assignments. He was also very outspoken in class and denounced the tradition of learning Talmud as quaint and old fashioned."

Rabbi Wein handled the complaint as he usually does when confronted initially with a thorny problem. He ignored it.

"I like to call it finessing the situation," he admits. In the afternoon, the secular studies Principal asked Rabbi Wein if he had suspended the boy in question. When he answered in the negative, the Principal sighed, "Well, then, I wonder where he's been for the last two weeks?"

Clearly matters had gone beyond the finessing stage, so Rabbi Wein tracked the boy down and they had an interview. "This was a problem I couldn't pretend wasn't there."

Rabbi Wein explained what happened next: "I make it a point to vent my anger in harmless ways. I remember reading how Abraham Lincoln dealt with his anger. Whenever he was personally attacked, he would never retaliate in public. What he did was sit down and write a response with as much fire and hatefulness that he could muster, attacking his enemies mercilessly. When he felt purged of his inner fury, he signed the letter, addressed and sealed the envelope. He then threw the envelope into a special drawer in his writing desk to remain there undelivered forever. By the middle of the Civil War the desk was crammed with undelivered letters.

"I, too, follow such a ritual. I have always written letters and placed them in my desks. There are letters in desks written in Miami Beach, Chicago, New York and now in Monsey (a lot in Monsey). After my interview with this young man I decided to write a letter to his parents. In it, I said it all: 'The boy is immature; he's rebellious; he belongs elsewhere; he's a negative influence on the others, etc.'

When my anger subsided, I felt slightly better, so I told my secretary to file it with the other unsent letters. This was another candidate for the Abe Lincoln drawer.

"In the interim, I hooked the boy up with a special teacher, for Talmud. We also reassigned him to a new learning partner. The English teachers were alerted to make allowances for the missed time and we gave him a tutor to catch up with the English classes. I instructed the dorm counselor to spend some extra time with him and try to get him back on the straight and narrow. By the end of the week the new program seemed to be working. He was reported to be less rebellious and by Friday of the following week his world and our world were no longer on a collision course.

"I was called out of town and had to spend *Shabbos* in another city. When I returned the following week," the Rabbi continued, "I saw the letter I had written on my desk. I was about to throw it into my 'Monsey drawer' when I noticed that this letter was a copy. I called in my secretary and asked her where the original was.

" 'Oh, I mailed the original last week,' she answered sweetly. 'That's the copy you wanted for your files.' "

Rabbi Wein gasped, "I didn't want that letter mailed."

He quickly thought of ways to reduce the damage. "I thought of calling the family and telling them to destroy the letter, to burn it. I thought of telling the boy to call his parents and tell them to disregard the letter. I thought of a lot of things, but as usual I did what I typically do in response to a yeshiva crisis. I sat back and waited for developments.

"I didn't hear from the parents for two whole months. By Passover, the boy made a significant recovery. He had a better attitude toward his teachers and was learning strongly. One day in May we received the infamous letter back in the office. The secretary made sure I saw it as soon as I came into the office. The envelope was stamped: UNDELIVERABLE AT THIS ADDRESS. The boy lived in New Jersey; the smudged, aged envelope read 'New York.' "

Moral: Rosh yeshivas need divine intervention, too.

Vocational Guidance

Rabbi Wein always looks at life from an historical perspective. He sees the trends, the fads, the styles that fade in and out of society like so many clouds in the April sky. When advising his young men on choosing their careers, he is very emphatic in pointing out that what was last year's six figure salary is next year's unemployment check. Nobody is selling junk bonds anymore, or designing Star Wars systems.

One field, however, that is forever looking for young, opportunistic individuals is the service industry — the service of the Jewish people. Torah leaders are always in demand. But, unfortunately, many people are not seeking this type of job.

For them, Rabbi Wein issues a strong warning: "No career is a sure thing, neither in terms of money, nor in terms of happiness. I know a fellow who went to medical school, became an intern, then a resident and when it came time to open his own practice, he came to me sobbing. 'I hate it,' he cried. He had entered the field for all the wrong reasons: prestige, parents, image. So at thirty-two years of age he started all over and now he is selling insurance, but at least he is happy. Unfortunately, it cost him ten years of his life."

Rabbi Wein's favorite story on job counseling is about a friend from the Chicago Yeshiva. As the boys approached their late teens, they were anxious to make the decisions that would shape the rest of their lives. There were no *kolels* (advanced Torah institutions supplying living stipends) at the time and even rabbinical positions were rare. If the boys hoped to get married and support a family, their days in the yeshiva were numbered. They would have to settle into professions or businesses and devote time for appropriate training. As Rabbi Wein is fond of saying, "There are no free lunches."

But one young man did not feel bound to this philosophy. He had a sure thing going. His family owned the largest seat cover manufacturing business in the United States. His grandfather was a millionaire and his father was president of the company. He was heir to this great business. The rest of the boys worked very hard in school because they knew yeshiva life would not last forever, but he took things easy. He lacked the urgency that drove the rest to finish one more page, one more *Tosafos*.

Rabbi Wein tells it this way, "I know none of you have ever heard of seat covers. But when I was growing up in Chicago, immediately after you bought a car you took it in to be fitted for seat covers. Driving in a car without seat covers was like eating at a table without a tablecloth. But by the 1960's that all changed. People stopped buying seat covers — I have no idea why. The family business went broke in less than five years. Suddenly, my friend had no fortune, no business, no job.

"Years later, on a visit to Chicago I saw him working behind the counter of a deli. I thought he had gone into the meat business because in my eyes he was always the wealthy one (I forgot he went broke). I entered the store to say hello and complimented him on his very successful delicatessen. He turned white, 'Are you making fun of me?' he asked. 'I work here for five dollars an hour.'

"I was terribly embarrassed by the incident but what a lesson it was. If you would have told him thirty years earlier that he would be packing sandwiches for a living, he would have laughed in your face. Yet it is the Almighty who does the laughing in this world. We plan our careers and He just sits back and allows time to mock our foolishness.

"Mensch tracht, und Gott lacht, ("Man plans and God laughs.") If we would only remember this before running off to medical school."

Satisfaction Guaranteed

Recently, Shaarei Torah sent out Pesach tapes of Rabbi Wein's speeches in an effort to raise money for his yeshiva, Shaarei Torah.

There were two one-hour taped speeches in each package and

the professional fundraiser who supervised the operation estimated that a typical donation would probably average $36. So when the yeshiva office got a check for $5,000 everyone was a little surprised. Rabbi Wein remarked that even *his* tapes are not that good. He instructed his staff to call the person identified on the check and ask him if a mistake had been made.

One of the secretaries knew that such a check would enable them to cover that day's fiscal shortfall and suggested that first they deposit the check and then do the detective work. Rabbi Wein demurred, "If we put it in the bank and it turns out to be a mistake, we'll never cover." And so the search began.

There are three yeshivas in the New York metropolitan area which have similar names to Shaarei Torah, two are in Brooklyn and one is in Jersey. The name on the check sounded Syrian so Rabbi Wein felt it must be one of the Shaarei Torahs in Brooklyn which cater to a Sephardic clientele. Sure enough, after about an hour of calling around Brooklyn they located the donor and he admitted that the check was his.

Indeed, there was a mixup. His secretary mailed the $5,000 check to Monsey when it was really designated for the building fund of a school of the same name in Brooklyn, and a check for $36 for the Rabbi Wein tapes was sent to the Brooklyn Shaarei Torah by mistake. Rabbi Wein thanked the donor anyway for his generosity and asked him if wanted the check returned to him or forwarded to the correct yeshiva.

The man answered, "Just keep it."

But Rabbi Wein protested, "But why? we all know it was a mistake."

The man had a ready answer, "If it got into your hands, it was no mistake. Keep it. God must have intended you to have it."

The donation, though inadvertent, was purely motivated. Rabbi Wein reflected, "The man didn't even ask for a plaque."

The Sura Yeshiva

In 1968, the last remaining Jews in Iraq were expelled from the country and sent to Israel. The Iraqis closed down all Jewish institutions, including the yeshiva at Sura that had been open since the time of the Second Temple, approximately 300 B.C.E. This school was the oldest educational institution in the world. Oxford University, the oldest secular institution, is barely 900 years old.

The Sura Yeshiva operated continuously for 2300 years. When Rabbi Wein related this fact to a group of his congregants, one of them said in pragmatic fashion, "Can you imagine what the deficit must have been?"

God's Sense of Humor

When Rabbi Wein was a student, one of the learning partners assigned to him was an excellent student. However, when it came to getting up in the morning, his friend was a total incompetent. A habitual oversleeper, he had great trouble bestirring himself in time for the *minyan*. Rabbi Wein would drop by his house on the way to *minyan* to resurrect him but to no avail. Around the yeshiva he was famous for his late entrances; not once, for example, did he make it to morning prayers on time to receive an *aliyah* (call up to the Torah).

At a recent yeshiva reunion, Rabbi Wein found out that his erstwhile learning partner had married well and made a nice life for himself; only life had played a trick on him. He worked for his father-in-law who had a fresh produce business buying and selling vegetables in the wholesale market. It was a profitable enterprise but he had to pay a price. To be successful in this business he had to be on hand at three o'clock in the morning to take delivery of incoming produce.

At the dinner, Rabbi Wein cajoled his friend, "You have to be there at what time? God is getting even for all those late prayers, eh?"

His friend replied, "There are compensations; on my lunch hour I attend an early *(naitz) minyan* in the neighborhood. Inasmuch as I'm the first one to arrive and they can rely on me, they made me *gabbai*. Now I assign all the *aliyos,* and if you come in late you don't get one."

Rabbi Wein uses this incident to philosophize: "God may not have a sense of humor, but he does have a funny way of getting even. We all have private demons; that's part of life. How we deal with them is what we are; and if we don't deal with them, don't think they are forgotten."

Kavod

When he discusses the topic of *kavod* (honor, respect for a person's importance) or the denial of *kavod*, Rabbi Wein likes to point to examples of Biblical figures. They understood that success depended on relinquishing one's self-importance. Moses was chosen to lead the Children of Israel while he was looking for a small lost sheep. Joshua was chosen his successor because, the Sages tell us, he cleaned up the *beis medrash* (study hall) after Moses had finished giving lecture. In the following anecdote, Rabbi Wein uses a modern Torah figure to illustrate his point.

"When he began the Telshe Yeshiva in Cleveland, Rabbi Eliyahu Mayer Bloch looked at the institution's financial situation and realized that the school could not afford a janitor. So he took the job. He would walk around the halls picking up trash off the floor and checking the building for problems. Rav Bloch had huge pockets sewn into his *kapotah* (frock coat) where he hid his tools. He would wander around the school building looking very much like its dean, when suddenly he would pull out a screwdriver and tighten the hinges on a door.

Once he was traveling in a car along with several prominent Torah figures headed for an important educational convention. As the Rabbis exchanged words of Torah they heard a pop, followed by a bumping — a flat tire. They pulled the car over and looked at each other. Immediately, Rav Bloch hopped out of his seat, took off his coat, loosened his tie and went to work. In ten minutes he had changed the tire. He even continued the conversation on the Talmud as he loaded the flat into the trunk.

Rabbi Wein expressed his great respect. "These men did it all, and they didn't stand on ceremony. They knew who they were and didn't need to be given *kavod*. That's why it was a pleasure to be around them."

> *One of the editor's earliest memories was watching Rabbi Moshe Feinstein policing the halls of his yeshiva, Mesifta Tiferes Yerushalaim (M.T.J.) on East Broadway on the lower East Side. When he spotted a piece of paper on the floor, Rav Moshe would pick it up and stuff it into his pocket. At the end of the day his pockets would bulge and he would have to be reminded to empty them before he went home.*

The Odd Couple

Once upon a time in America, immediately after The War, two rabbis, alumni of a very famous yeshiva in Lithuania, found themselves working together in a small midwestern yeshiva. One, who had been rabbi in a prominent yeshiva in Lithuania, was the eighth grade teacher, and the other, who had been the *mashgiach* in the same yeshiva, was now in charge of the fifth grade. When they met at the beginning of the school year, they embraced each other warmly and renewed their relationship. During the year they recalled 'the way it was.' Happily met, they gave each other encouragement and felt how fortunate they were to have found continuity in an American yeshiva.

The tragic uprooting from Europe left its scars, though. They compared notes many times. The *mashgiach* had been stranded in America on a fundraising tour when the Germans invaded Poland. To save his large family, he smuggled forged passports to them in the hope the Nazis would let them emigrate to South America. However, the papers just delayed the inevitable, and the family was shipped to Bergen-Belsen for "processing" in 1943. They were not heard from again. A few years later, in America, the *mashgiach* remarried and joined the faculty of this small yeshiva in the midwest.

His friend, a much younger man, escaped because he happened to be visiting at the Mir Yeshiva with his family in the spring of 1941 and was miraculously swept out of harm's way, through Russia, in the frenzied days before Poland fell.

They traced events in America and discovered that many of their colleagues in their pre-war European yeshiva had also escaped. At the end of the semester, they resolved to reestablish an American version of their old Lithuanian yeshiva using as many of the old faculty as they could find. "What a triumph for Torah," they thought.

And so they started what was to become a major Torah

institution. They hired many of their old faculty, rented another building in town, borrowed the necessary money, forswore their salaries until the school could get on its feet and finally opened a replica of their old yeshiva. At the outset it had no advanced classes, but the traditions of its old yeshiva sustained it and in that merit it grew successful — an American yeshiva in the European tradition.

In those days there were many problems facing yeshiva administrators: finances, staffing, finances, anti-Semitism, finances, secular influences, etc. The yeshivas reflected the problems of a tiny minority trying to rebuild itself from the ashes of Europe. These two school administrators, however, were able to stave off failure. Their skills and temperaments complemented each other perfectly. The *ex-mashgiach*, now the yeshiva dean, was the overall director of education and he was uncompromising in his efforts to create an authentic European-style Torah institution. He imbued the yeshiva with a spirit of high seriousness and each student understood "learning" was the main order of business. Under his vigilant supervision this yeshiva was no place to fool around.

The younger rabbi was different. He had a charming personality and projected an image of serene affability. A witty raconteur, he was a superb peacemaker. Where the older Dean was confrontational, the younger rabbi tried to heal rifts before they got started. The Dean recognized his talents and used him to mediate conflicts whenever his own style drew fire. The rabbis were the perfect blend of drive and finesse.

The men divided labor according to their abilities. Every year like clockwork, the young rabbi, now called the chief administrator, somehow managed to raise $500,000, just enough to cover the deficit. In those days raising such a sum of money was a heroic feat. For his part, the Dean managed to recruit students, deal with curriculum, counsel parents, supervise daily operations, and still give four classes a day. He built the yeshiva from the inside, the fundraiser from the outside, and their efforts stretched human endurance.

But theirs was not a complete harmony. They had one major ongoing dispute which centered on a difference in admission policy.

According to the Dean, the purpose of a yeshiva was to produce scholars. He insisted that only the best boys be admitted, and he instituted an entrance test that would screen out less able students. As the head educator, he felt this was the way in which the best yeshivas in Europe went, and an American yeshiva should not settle for less.

As the chief administrator and fundraiser, the younger man disagreed with this point of view. In America, he argued, "We need to serve a diversity of students, many kinds of boys from many types of families. There is no telling what the next generation will need or who we will have to teach ten years from now."

The yeshiva Dean listened to this argument but was unconvinced. "We need quality," he told his compatriot. "We cannot dilute our Talmudic program." To his thinking, only the best need apply and only the best of the best were to be sent forth.

The fundraising rabbi, always the pragmatist, pointed out problems. "We cannot make a yeshiva just for the sons of other rabbis; in America we need to produce many students to replace the ones we lost in the Holocaust. When Torah learning has suffered such a loss, we cannot raise our standards too high. We need all we can get." He paused to see if his argument was being absorbed. "Besides," he concluded, "we can't just cater to the sons of rabbis — we need people who can pay the full tuition!"

The yeshiva Dean couldn't hold back a half-smile. As usual, his colleague was partially right — he was making good sense. Reluctantly, they reached a practical solution which accommodated both points of view. The administrator could conduct some of the admissions testing, but the Dean reserved the final decision for himself. "You send me what you like, but I'm going to have the final veto — with no override." And that's how they left it, a divided vision but a workable process.

For years, the admission arrangement held, but each educator clung to his rights and would not surrender his vision. They struggled every year, sometimes bitterly, to graft their ideas onto the character of the yeshiva. But the potentially divisive split in philosophy never ripped the school apart. On the contrary, as the men wrestled with one another the competition served to infuse the school with a fiery intensity. And so they fought for their version of excellence, two strong-minded men battling to define the character of Jewish education in the American midwest.

The conflict was resolved in an unusual way. One day, the administrator, returning from a fundraising trip to New Jersey, was about to report to his boss when he heard the most pitiable crying from the other side of the yeshiva Dean's office door. It was unmistakably the crying of the Dean. He told the secretaries to leave for an early lunch hour while he remained in his outer office guarding his friend's privacy.

After about ten minutes of soul-rending sobbing, the Dean opened his door slightly and signaled for his colleague to enter. His black suit jacket was torn from the breast pocket to the edge of the collar.

"What's the matter, Rabbi, what's wrong?"

He spoke slowly at first, "Of course, you know that I was married and had a large family in Europe." The administrator nodded.

"Did you know I never said *kaddish* (the mourners' prayer) for them.?"

"Yes, I did."

"Did you know why?"

Lowering himself to the ground, the venerable yeshiva Dean started to whimper. As if talking to the pool of tears which was accumulating on the floor, he explained, "For over ten years I tried to say *kaddish* for my family — my wife and my children. I knew they were gone but deep inside me I still held out the hope that someday one of them would survive and come back to me. I tried to say *kaddish*, but I didn't say it, not once."

He paused, then looked up into the younger rabbi's eyes, "Today, I thought about them and I realized that I didn't remember some of my children's names. Now they are truly gone. I will now begin to recite *kaddish* for them."

"Is there anything I can do, Rabbi?" inquired the younger man.

The yeshiva Dean replied, "Please tell my wife to prepare my house for the period of mourning. I will be sitting *shivah* this entire week."

"Is there anything else, Rabbi?"

"Yes. I want the school to run differently. Perhaps I've been too stubborn — too stubborn personally and too stubborn for the school." The Dean paused to allow his colleague to absorb the thought.

He continued, "I held out for the return of my family for many years. Against all reason I held out. I tried to deny what happened to me. I tried to hold on to what I could. I think I did the same thing with the yeshiva."

"Therefore, I've decided to open the gates. For the new semester I won't be exercising my veto regularly anymore. We need to rebuild the Jewish people, and we need all the students we can help. We must close the chapter on Europe."

The younger man heard the message clearly, "I'll only admit the best of the best, Rabbi. Anyway," he said, "that's all we have left," and then he sat down next to his friend to console him in his pain.

The destiny of American Jewry floated on the tears and heartache of men like these — not so oddly matched after all.

6

Israel and the Holocaust

A large percentage of Nazi death camp commandants had Ph.D.'s or M.D.'s — knowledge is not synonymous with goodness.

Sign on the road to the Western Wall: V'kiru levavchem, v'al bigdeichem. ("Don't tear your clothes; tear your hearts.")

Israel and the Holocaust

n the preface to his definitive history, *The Holocaust,* Martin Gilbert describes a journey he made in 1959, to the Nazi death camp, Treblinka:

❦ ❦ ❦

From Treblinka village we proceeded for another mile or two, along the line of an abandoned railway through a forest of tall trees. Finally we reached an enormous clearing, bounded on all sides by dense woodland. Darkness was falling, and with it, the chill of night and a cold dew. I stepped down . . . to the sandy soil: a soil that was gray rather than brown. Driven by I know not what impulse, I ran my hand through that soil, again and again. The earth beneath my feet was coarse and sharp, filled with the fragments of human bone.

The world will try to revise and even obliterate the story of what took place in the killing camps of Treblinka, Matthausen, Auschwitz, Bergen-Belsen, Buchenwald, Dachau, Bitberg, etc. The world is built on falsity and will try to trample on truth. It will try to make one believe that nothing consequential took place to the Jewish people in Europe in the years 1939-45. That effort has already begun.

Therefore, no account of Jewish affairs should be published without acknowledging that the earth beneath our feet is filled with "fragments of human bone."

Mama

Several years ago, Rabbi Wein went to Israel. As part of the touring package, his travel agent booked him into the Jerusalem Plaza for three days. His room was on the fourteenth floor and had a magnificent view of the Old City. It was mid-December and the *intifada* was raging into its second year. Tourists had canceled their travel plans to Israel and the Holy City was empty. Nobody was in town, except, that is, for the fourteenth floor of the Plaza. There the "joint was jumping."

A church group from Appleton, Wisconsin was making its annual pilgrimage to Israel. The Rabbi couldn't avoid the group as he waited for the elevator to take him downstairs. They were so enthusiastic about their touring plans, they were hard to ignore. To tell the truth, the Rabbi rather enjoyed their presence. On the trips down the elevator he looked forward to hearing their midwestern accents. It was comforting, a little piece of the 'old sod.' After all, Chicago (his home town) borders Wisconsin.

"Are you an Orthodox Rabbi?" The question was directed at him from the center of the elevator. It was from the Protestant minister who served as the tour leader. The elevator reached the lobby and Rabbi Wein timed his answer so he could make a quick getaway.

"Yes, I didn't know it was so obvious."

The minister followed the Rabbi as he darted through the lobby and slid through the revolving doors. Now with both of them outside the hotel he persisted.

"I've never met an Orthodox Rabbi before. All we have in Wisconsin are mostly Conservatives and a few Reform. I'd really like to get your point of view on things."

Rabbi Wein didn't want to appear rude but the last thing he needed to do that morning was discuss theology with an assiduous cleric. "Maybe later we can sit down and talk, now I've got an appointment." However, the cleric was very insistent and spoke briefly with the Rabbi in the lobby. In their short interchange, it became clear that although the minister knew little about Orthodoxy, he knew a great deal about the *Tanach* and could quote extensively from Biblical sources. Rabbi Wein admired his erudition but, realizing he was behind schedule, cut the discussion short. "Perhaps we'll talk later, but right now I must go" he said and left the lobby and hopped into the first taxi on the waiting line.

The minister agreed to desist but walked a few steps out into the street in the wake of the departing cab and shouted, "I'll be looking for you." There was something in the tone of his voice that made Rabbi Wein uncomfortable.

On his trips to Israel, Rabbi Wein usually finds that he is

overbooked with speaking engagements and can hardly find time to relax. So for the next few days, every time the Rabbi was solicited by the minister, he found good reason to evade lengthy interviews. However, in the few exchanges he did have, he discovered that his pursuer was also an expert in the Hebrew language and knew quite a bit about modern Jewish history.

On the evening of his flight back to the States, Rabbi Wein got down early to catch his cab to Ben Gurion Airport. In the lobby he decided to get something to eat in the coffee shop before departing. There the leader of the Christians was waiting for him.

"I would enjoy your company for coffee. Would you please join me?" The heartiness of his request belied the lateness of the hour. He was fresh and poised for the encounter as if had been there in planned ambush. It was very hard to turn him down. There wasn't another soul in the shop.

The Rabbi sat down and hoped the questioning would be painless.

To his surprise the minister restricted himself to current events, albeit with an exasperated tone.

"On our tour of Bethlehem our bus was stoned by an Arab."

"What do you think of all this? How is it going to end? The violence just goes on and on. There doesn't seem to be an end in sight." The Rabbi said he was sorry it happened.

The minister continued. "I wonder what the Orthodox position on this violence is? What do you think, Rabbi, what's going to happen to Israel? Things are getting out of hand, aren't they?"

The Rabbi could sense the cleric's frustration. He knew Americans have no appetite for unresolved wars. He tried to finesse the barrage.

"First let me tell you that God hasn't spoken to me in at least two weeks. So I don't know what's going to happen here. All I know is that Israel is a place where the unexpected happens; it is a holy place governed by hidden rules."

This didn't comfort his compatriot. Rabbi Wein tried again to lighten the moment and provide some perspective. "Tell me, thirty years ago, what would the odds have been that we would be having this conversation regarding this topic in this location?" Rabbi Wein was about to continue when he noticed that his acquaintance was not pleased by the lighthearted direction the Rabbi was taking.

Visibly agitated, the minister now went on the attack, and in a strident tone asked, "What's going to happen with all this rock throwing, this violence? Things have changed drastically since the *intifada* began. Your army is shooting down children. Over three hundred Palestinians have been killed, and the world is against you now! What is it that you Jews really want?" The minister had raised the pitch of questioning to a new level and it was getting very warm in the air-conditioned coffee shop.

The Rabbi felt that the time for "Twenty Questions" was over; now it was time for a Jewish history lesson. He picked up the gauntlet that had been thrown and told his tale simply but sharply.

"Let me relate a story that might give you an insight into what we Jews really want. It's an episode from a book called *The Holocaust* by Martin Gilbert. The book is over 900 pages long, but I'm just going to paraphrase an excerpt from one page. Eliezer Melamed, a survivor, is the witness to this story. It takes place in 1942 in the Polish city of Stolpce:

Rabbi Wein paraphrased Melamed's story, "In the fall the Jewish ghetto was surrounded by German soldiers and Panzer tanks. Death pits were being dug right before the residents' eyes. Where could the Jews hide? ... in cellars, in attics — they sewed themselves into feather blankets — anywhere they could. The Germans entered the ghetto shooting and searching. When they were finished they started to burn the houses behind them.

"A mother and her three children were hiding in one of these houses — the mother hid in one corner of the room and the children behind sacks in another.

"Upon entering the room, the Germans discovered the children, and quickly pulled them out. One of the children, a young boy began to scream, 'Mama, Mama!' But another of them, around the age of four, shouted to his brother in Yiddish, '*Zog nit Mameh, men vet ir oich zunemen.*' (Don't say Mama, they'll take her too.)

"The boy stopped screaming. The mother remained silent as her children were dragged away. The mother was saved. As she watched her children being dragged away by the Germans she was hitting her head against the wall, as if to punish herself for remaining silent, for wanting to live.

"What do we Jews really want?" The Rabbi restated the minister's question. "Well, I'll tell you what I want. All I want is that my grandchildren should be able to call 'Mama.' All we want is the world should leave us alone."

Without waiting for his reply, Rabbi Wein left the coffee shop. The minister stared mutely at his cup of coffee, speechless for the first time since he arrived in Israel.

Yad Vashem

Five years ago, *Yad Vashem*, the Israeli Holocaust Museum in Jerusalem, opened a new wing. It was financed with several million dollars from a wealthy Jewish family named Spiegel living in Southern California. The wing was dedicated to the one and a half million children under twelve who were slaughtered by the Nazis. The list of innocents includes the donor's son.

Rabbi Wein went to see the museum and its new addition. "I had seen Holocaust memorials all over the world and I was expecting to see the standard exhibit full of pictures, personal accounts, gruesome statistics," Rabbi Wein said. "I was not prepared to step into the addition the Spiegel family erected.

"I walked into a single enormous underground room. It was so dark I could not see my hand in front of my face," he said. "In the middle of the room a single burning candle provided a small dot of light. Mirrors cunningly placed around the room bounced the light of that candle everywhere, transforming one point of light into hundreds of tiny flames. It was a congregation of tiny souls in search of bodies.

"When I walked into that room," Rabbi Wein recalled, "I was enveloped by darkness. My eyes focused on the small dots of light, which did nothing to illuminate the room. They were suspended in midair. Then I heard the recorded voice of a man speaking to the visitors. He said nothing profound yet his words struck deeply into my heart. I stood in the blackest of rooms and stared at the light. I began to imagine that I was surrounded by a million and a half children:

"'Chaim Smolovitz,' said the disembodied monotone, 'Vilna, eight years old. Sarah Kleiner, Vilna, eleven years old. David Ratner, Warsaw, four years old. Rosa Klepper, Berlin, seven years old . . .' the voice read names without an end. Moishe, Ferencz, Alexander, Shaindy, Zipporah, David, Joel, Zoltan . . . hundreds of thousands of names, taken from the lists of the Holocaust victims which the Nazis recorded so meticulously. These were names of Jews who would have been in their forties and fifties today with children and grandchildren of their own. Names, names, names until I could bear it no longer.

"I never cried so hard in my life," Rabbi Wein continued. "I fled into the blinding Jerusalem sun. Then it occurred to me that they did not call my name. I'm of that age; my name could have been on that list. I just happened to live in Chicago, not Europe. Had my grandfather moved east instead of west, my name could have been on that roster.

"And if I escaped, there is a reason for it. God saved me because I have a special purpose. Therefore, I have to increase my efforts to do something positive for the Jewish people. I don't know what I should do, build more yeshivas, talk to more Jews, write articles, but I cannot rest until I contribute to the cause of Jewish redemption. I was spared for a reason."

※ ※ ※

14-year-old Berel Wein attended yeshiva in Chicago, Illinois. One day, a middle-aged man entered his class, and the Rebbe signaled for everybody to stand. The man spoke a few words in Yiddish and left. The class did not know who he was and did not understood what he had said. He was not introduced as a great scholar or even as a rabbi. Why did they have to stand? The Rebbe told them simply, "There are certain people in this world who have done noteworthy things for the Jewish people. The Talmud calls them *anshei ma'aseh*, 'men of deeds,' men who have done something important. The man who just spoke here is such a man. He saved fifty Jewish lives. For these men one must stand."

❈ ❈ ❈

"Hitler had a collection of every Jewish artifact: ark curtains, menorahs, *siddurs*, Megillahs, spice boxes, *bris milah* knives, *shechitah* knives, etc. because, he said, 'When there are no more Jews in the world we're going to have a museum to show what once was.'

"But we're not big on museums," Rabbi Wein says, "we are the museum ourselves."

Emperor Hadrian

In 1988, the Israeli Museum sponsored a traveling exhibition of its religious and historical treasures. At the New York Metropolitan Museum of Art we were able to view the greatest collection of Israeli art and archaeology in the world.

One of the chief treasures on display was a great bronze statue of the Roman emperor, Hadrian. In the year 137 C.E., he put down the rebellion of Bar Kochba, executed the great Rabbi Akiva in Caesaria and attempted to destroy the Jewish people and their religion.

This marvelously preserved statue of Hadrian occupies a central and elevated position in the exhibition hall. The voice of the Director of the Museum, which is on the tape recorder the museum rents for the tour, explains that this statue is the only representation of Hadrian which exists in the world today. It's not in Rome, or in any other city in the world. If you want to know what that vile man looked like, you have to see this statue, courtesy of the Israeli Minister of Art and Antiquities.

He stands alone, absolutely lifelike, his bronzed head surveying the army of tourists who stare at him. The voice of Thomas Hoving, the Director, announces, "It is an irony of history that he enjoys benign captivity in the permanent exhibit of the Israel Museum in Jerusalem, Israel, the homeland of a people he devoted over three years of his life to destroy."

Rabbi Wein loves to highlight the twists of fate that make the study of Jewish history such a rewarding endeavor. He led a Bais Torah contingent on a tour of the exhibit one Sunday and stated, "Only the Almighty, with His exquisite irony, could have invented such an interesting unraveling of events."

Persians and Nazis

Rabbi Wein: "In an effort to destroy Judaism, the Persians banned the recitation of the *Shema* (central Jewish prayer). They posted guards at the doors of the synagogues to prevent its reading. They also prohibited the weekly reading from the Torah.

"In response to the ban on the *Shema*, the Jews moved it from the Shabbos morning service to the *kedushah* of the *Mussaf* service. The guards were listening for the *Shema* during the regular service and when they didn't hear it, they left the synagogue without waiting for *Mussaf*.

"In response to the elimination of the weekly Torah portion, the Jews tried to substitute some Scripture to replace the banned Torah chapter. They negotiated with the Persians, asking permission to read from the Prophets. For reasons which are not clear to us, the Persians agreed to the request.

"It appears from history that the Persians were fond of promulgating all kinds of edicts and regulations. However, in this case the officials got carried away and forgot the intent of the original decree. To their minds the Jews were forbidden to read from the Torah and not from the Prophets. In this respect they resembled modern, bureaucratic governments, intent on carrying out the letter of the law and ignoring its spirit."

Rabbi Wein points out the similarity of the Persians to the Third Reich:

"During the Second World War, the German government sent Rabbi Joseph Breuer, the spiritual leader of the Jewish community in Washington Heights, a monthly check for serving in the German Army as a chaplain during the first World War. Reaching the age of 65, Rabbi Breuer was entitled to his veteran's pension. "If he would have been in Germany they would have put him in the furnace but since he was in New York they sent him checks because 'rules are rules.' Rabbi Wein reiterates, "In Germany the furnace, in New York checks; that is the insanity of bureaucracy."

> As a footnote to the Persian episode, Rabbi Wein adds: "The Jews, for their part, are great conservatives; they treasure custom." Rabbi Wein concludes, "When the Persian decree fell away and the Jews were free to read from the Torah itself, they decided to lengthen the service by retaining the reading of the Prophets, too. In addition, when they saw that the Persians were not enforcing their edict prohibiting the recitation of Shema in the Mussaf service, they added some statements to the Kedushah which contained oblique hopes ('rachamov shainis') that they would outlast their oppressors. We say these even today. The Kedushah should only contain the recitation, "Kadosh, Kadosh, Kadosh, Hashem tzevokos m'lo col ha'aretz kevodo," and the verse, "Boruch k'vod malchuso l' olum vaed." That is the

whole Kedushah; everything else is extraneous. However, the Jews can't help themselves. They always take revenge against their enemies, even if it is only liturgical. It's our way of reminding ourselves that we're here to stay.

Herzl and the Kaiser

In the early days of this century, Theodore Herzl asked the Kaiser, the leader of the Austro-Hungarian Empire, what the chances were of the Jews gaining Palestine as a homeland.

The Kaiser snickered and replied, "Mr. Herzl, three major empires would have to fall before you would be allowed to struggle for Palestine. Its present occupier, the Ottoman Empire, would have to be defeated. Czarist Russia, which guarantees Jerusalem for the Eastern Orthodox Church, would have to capitulate, and the German Empire, which guarantees Palestine for the Christian Church, would have to collapse. Of course, the British Empire, which controls the Suez, would have to share its sphere of influence with you Jews, too. And that, Herr Hezel, cannot happen."

By 1920, a scant twenty years later, two of the three empires collapsed and the British Empire issued the Balfour Declaration. In W.W. II Germany, the third empire, was defeated; no longer a power in the Middle East. In 1900, what were the odds of that happening?

We Jews consistently sell ourselves short. We must learn to believe in our destiny guided by our Divine Protector. The future is there for all to see. I can't understand Jews who invest millions of dollars in Florida condominiums," Rabbi Wein often wonders, "but won't buy a single dwelling in *Eretz Yisroel*. Investment in *Eretz Yisroel* is gilt edged."

❦ ❦ ❦

Rabbi Wein expands on the above theme:

"A Russian Jew named Wissotzky once owned the tea concession for the Czar's entire military operation. Since the Czar's armies numbered in the millions and tea drinking was a daily Russian custom, this concession made Wissotzky very rich. One day Wissotzky was approached by the World Zionist Organization to invest in the tea business in Israel. Wissotzky laughed at this preposterous idea. The Turks governed Palestine and they were notoriously difficult to deal with. Besides, he pointed out, Palestine cannot produce its own tea and tea leaves from India were too costly to import."

"The Zionists assured him that they would solve all the problems. They were so persuasive he finally sent enough money to start a small tea business. In 1917 the Czar and his army were swept from power. The communists seized all the businesses the Czar had franchised, including Mr. Wissotzky's tea business. After the revolution the only asset he owned was the small company he set up in Palestine before the revolution. He fled there and rebuilt his business. To this day, eighty years later, his Israeli company is still selling tea under the Wissotzky label.

"There are many variations on this. A man I knew owned property in downtown Havana before Castro took over. It was worth millions. When the State of Israel was formed in 1948, he bought some Israel bonds 'as an act of charity,' since he thought its investment value was nil. Little did he know that he needed those bonds to start over when he was forced by Castro to leave Cuba in a hurry."

Rabbi Wein summarizes: "A *dirah* (dwelling) in Jerusalem or a condo in Boca? Which will your grandchildren live in?"

One More Generation

In 1948, when Ben Gurion established the first cabinet in the State of Israel, he gave representation to everyone. It was in the middle of the War of Independence and he didn't have time for politics. He included all the political parties in his government, except the Communist Party. As part of the deal to include even the religious parties, he agreed that the Israeli Army would be kept totally kosher.

The head of the left wing party, the Mapam, a man by the name of Yaari, whose son later sat in jail for spying for Russia, came to Ben Gurion and protested the concession to the religious party, "Why are you selling out? We've been fighting for fifty years to have a secular state and now we have finally achieved one and you make the army kosher! Why don't you fight them on this issue? Besides we don't really need their support; we can get along without them." He added, "Why should my children have to eat kosher?"

Ben Gurion answered him, "Leave this issue alone. Time will solve it for us. In one more generation, the religious will disappear. They're an anachronism, they'll all be gone."

> Forty years later there is still a problem. The secular are well aware the religious are here to stay. And this realization sharpens the problem. When one believes a minority will fade away one can be tolerant; when one fears they're about to take over, panic strikes. That explains Israel today; the vehemence, the polarization, the verbal violence.

Private Benjamin

Rabbi Wein heard this story from an aide to Ben Gurion.

In Israel in 1952 one of the issues dividing the secular and the religious worlds was the drafting of women into the Army. There was an exemption provided for Orthodox women, but it was a bitter battle and it threatened to tear the society apart.

Ben Gurion himself felt there would be a *Kulturkampf,* and he didn't know what to do. He attempted to hold things together and calm everyone by courting the opposition publicly. He dressed himself up in a black hat and black suit and visited the leader of Orthodox Jewry, the great Chazon Ish, Rabbi Avraham Yeshaya Karelitz, who lived in Bnei Brak.

After they exchanged pleasantries, the Chazon Ish invited the Prime Minister in for a cup of tea, and they discussed the exemption. The Rabbi explained the problem this way: "The Talmud in *Bava Metziah* poses a problem: Suppose you have two camels going around the side of a mountain, and they come to a part of the road where there's room for only one camel to pass. Which camel has the right to pass first and which one must give way? The Talmud states that the camel with the greatest load takes priority and the other camel should give way."

The Chazon Ish continued, "Traditional Jewry has carried the biggest load for centuries. You just came on the scene four years ago and the State doesn't have much baggage yet. It seems to me that you have to give way a little. You must accommodate us. And if that means that the State of Israel will not violate the rights of our women and force them to serve, then that is what you'll have to do."

There is no record of Ben Gurion's response. But, later that week, the newspapers ran the story with Ben Gurion photographed wearing a big black hat on his visit to the apartment of the Chazon

Ish in Bnei Brak. The citizens of the State of Israel 'got the picture' and they too made their accommodation.

Stepping Out

When Rabbi Nachman Bulman, a prominent scholar and friend of Rabbi Wein, made *aliyah* to Israel he was taken for a walk down Yaffa Road in Jerusalem by Rav Eliyahu Kitov, the famous author of books on the Jewish religion. The spectacle of religious and irreligious parading down the street was very disconcerting to Rav Bulman. He turned to his friend and complained, "Look what's going on here. They dress so shamelessly; it's so chaotic a mixture!"

Rabbi Kitov grabbed him by the arm and commanded him to walk straight ahead, calling out each step as they took it: "*Aleph* (step one), *beis* (step two), *gimel* (step three), *dalet* (step four), *mitzvah*; *aleph*, *beis*, *gimel*, *dalet*, *mitzvah*; *aleph*, *bait*, *gimel*, *dalet*, *mitzvah*." The Talmud states that every four steps one walks in *Eretz Yisroel* is a *mitzvah*.

Having got the message, Rabbi Bulman was then able to walk down the street less incensed about the state of decorum.

Arab Zionists

"The Arabs are the strongest Zionists." So said Ben Gurion. According to Rabbi Wein this is what he meant: "They doubled Israel's population in the first ten years. They kicked the

Moroccan Jews out of Morocco, the Iraqi Jews out of Iraq, as well as expelling all the Tunisian, Egyptian, and Turkish Jews. If we had waited for the Jews to come of their own accord, we would still be waiting."

❈ ❈ ❈

"Why are the Arabs so important now? Our enemies must be stronger than we — we can't be opposed by a Class D ball team. We need to be opposed by Major Leaguers, preferably world class opponents. We never fought a fair fight. The cards were always stacked against us."

Miracles

Mr. Yitzchak Nissim was the Minister of Finance under Menachem Begin. He was instrumental in stopping the runaway inflation that was threatening to destroy the shaky Israeli economy.

At an international conference he was asked to explain how the economy works in his country. He tried to explain how the special conditions of the Israeli economy depended on so many complex variables that it defied logical analysis.

"If the truth were known," he admitted, "such an economy can only be run by *Nissim.*"

(In Hebrew, "Nissim" means miracles.)

The Sale

A couple that Rabbi Wein knows just made *aliyah* and bought an apartment. In Tel Aviv they went furniture shopping. In one store the couple dickered for over an hour with a furniture salesman, and couldn't make the salesman understand that they didn't want the French provincial mahogany table, but preferred the more modern formica table. The salesman kept dropping the price of his traditional piece, but it did no good and the couple insisted on the formica piece. Finally, the salesman gave in and wrote the order seemingly as the couple wished.

A week later, a truck rolled up to the couple's house and the table was brought up the stairs. After the couple unpacked it, they discovered the store had delivered the wrong table, the French Provincial table they didn't want. The husband called the salesman to complain.

The salesman listened to his complaint and said: "Why are you complaining? I knew you really wanted this one so I had them deliver it."

> *Rabbi Wein loves to say: "Why do I love Israel? Because it's so Jewish."*

The 1929 Riots

In 1929, the Arab mobs rioted against the Jewish population in Hebron and destroyed the Slobodka Yeshiva, killing thirty students in their murderous rampage. When word got out that they were on a pogrom, the Jews fled and hid wherever they could. One Yemenite Jew was hiding in a tree when the Arabs spotted him.

They ran to the tree and looked him over closely. He was dressed in Bedouin clothes and wore an Arab turban. One of the leaders of the squad declared, "He's one of us; let's get going."

The Taimani (Yemenite) was so insulted by the appraisal, he leaped out of the tree and shouted, *"Ani Yehudi, Ani Yehudi."* (I am a Jew, I am a Jew.) The death squad returned to run him down and stab him to death. He couldn't stand to be viewed as an Arab even to save his own life.

> *This is a very sharp story but it gives one some perspective on the history of the struggle with our cousins. As Rabbi Wein puts it, "There's no fight like a family fight."*

Halleluyah

Rabbi Wein was shopping for some silver gifts in a store on Rechov Yaffo in Jerusalem. The Taimani (Yemenite) proprietor who was waiting on the Rabbi took a telephone call in the back of the store, leaving the Rabbi to examine some of the merchandise alone. A few seconds later, the Rabbi heard a tremendous shout of exultation emanate from the back room. The Taimani retailer rushed into the display showroom and was shouting, *"Boruch Hashem, Boruch Hashem,"* (Thank God! Thank God!) embraced the Rabbi.

"Wish me a giant mazel tov — after six girls my wife just gave birth to a boy."

"Six girls — is that right? I almost know how you feel — what are their names?" asked Rabbi Wein.

The shopkeeper danced around the display cases singing their names, "The first was Gila, then came Reena, the third was Ditza, Hedvah the fourth, and then there were Ahava and Achva." (The names, all meaning joy, were taken directly from the verse of

"Seven Blessings.") He was dancing ecstatically turning little graceful circles in his small shop.

"Are you going to name your first boy Shalom?" (the next name in the verse.)

"No, b'ezrat Hashem (with the help of God). We're going to name him — Halleluyah!!!!!!!"

> Later, after he had settled down, the shopkeeper invited the Rabbi to the bris and explained the wisdom of the word "Mazel" (luck): "Mem (M) stands for mokom ('place,' i.e. God). zayen (Z) stands for zman (time) and lamed (L) stands for loshon (language). In other words, he explained, say the right words in the right place at the right time and you get Mazel."
>
> Such is Israel, a country with miraculous people unfolding into greatness under the abiding guidance of God, the right name (Israel) in the right place (where it has always been) at the right time (now). Halleluyah!!!!!!!

7
Golus In America

The best golus has been frei goyim (non-believing gentiles) and frum yidden (believing Jews). The worst has been frum goyim and frei yidden.

Golus In America

hile he was the Rav in a synagogue in Miami Beach, Rabbi Wein used to entertain various Torah personalities who visited from all over the world. One such visitor during the winter months was a rabbi who was recovering from heart surgery. Rabbi Wein befriended him and they became study partners, learning the Talmud every afternoon in Rabbi Wein's backyard.

On one such afternoon, as the ocean breezes wafted across Miami Beach, a beautiful golden bird perched on the branch of a grapefruit tree which hung over their *shtenders* (lecterns). It sang lovely melodies to accompany the learning. The visiting Rabbi looked up at the semi-tropical scene and commented, "If you're going to have to be in *golus*, Miami is not so bad."

The *golus* (exile) in America has been the kindest and most productive exile of all. We Jews have thrived in every respect. Who could have imagined an Agudah convention taking place in the paradise of Palm Springs or a Kosher Food Expo in a Manhattan convention center named after a Jewish Senator?

We march in the corridors of power as equals. We even have an Orthodox Senator and over twenty Jewish Congressmen. The freedoms granted us in this exile are unparalleled in history. It is Rabbi Wein's firm belief that the Almighty gave us America as a gift, a respite from the horrors of the War. But he warns, "Things may return to normal for us faster than we'd like to believe. Pretty soon we are going to be reminded that we are here only temporarily."

❦ ❦ ❦

A story which happened to him while in Florida hints of the transiency of the American *golus*.

"Once, we conducted a successful campaign to remodel our synagogue. We spent a lot of money to rehabilitate the outside of the main building. The contractor used a new spraying technique which combined stucco and cement in a liquid spray which was handsome and durable beyond belief. It also glittered in the sunlight as if the walls were overlaid with semiprecious stones.

"After the building was completed the novel surface attracted a great deal of attention. A very active public relations committee in the synagogue publicized the remodeling and we were interviewed by the media. Many pictures were taken of the refurbished facade and my synagogue was featured that week in the Miami Sunday newspapers, (in the "Architecture" and "Religion" sections). One day I received a phone call from a nun in an adjoining Catholic school who had read about the building and wanted to take her class to visit our synagogue. 'To see their Jewish brethren in their house of worship,' were her words.

"Such are the penalties of being the Rabbi of a synagogue in the public eye. It became my lot to escort the nun and her class on a guided tour. The children obviously were well prepared with good questions about architecture and Jewish ritual. They made the most of their opportunity to acquaint themselves with their 'Jewish brethren.' After a rather lengthy tour the nun made a request that gave me pause.

" 'Before we leave, we'd like to say a prayer in the synagogue,' she asked.

"I blanched. I felt I was possibly overstepping *halachah* by letting them visit in the first place and now they wanted to use the place to pray, too. No way!

"I was about to deny their request when the nun showed me the text she wanted to pray from. It was one of the Psalms (Psalm 23) written by King David. I was about to accede to her wish when I looked at her psalter again. The last line read, 'By the grace of the Father, the Son and the Holy Ghost and The Lord, J.C.'

" 'One minute,' I objected, 'this Psalm was written eight hundred years before your Lord. And it was a Psalm written by David, a Jewish King. The last line is not part of the Psalm. You may read that Psalm but with the authentic text.' I gave her the ArtScroll version."

"She inspected the *siddur* with its marvelous English translation facing the original Hebrew. I could see this was not going to be easy for her. 'I always thought that this Psalm ended with 'By the Father, the Son and the Holy Ghost,' she plaintively demurred. 'This is the way I was taught it in my Catholic elementary school.'

"I proceeded to show her various references which refuted her version of the authorship. 'I've been reading this Psalm for over thirty years,' she said, 'and I can't really change the way I've been taught. Maybe we'll just go home now and I'll get clarification from the bishop about the real author. I'll be back.' With that, she shuffled her charges silently out of the synagogue.

"I did receive a thank you note from her the next week, but no mention was made of the disputed text. I never saw them again during my tenure at that synagogue in Miami.

> In America, old synagogues become museums and old yeshivas become Chinese noodle warehouses, and, God spare us, old Psalms acquire new authors. They'll be back. No matter how many congressmen we have in Washington, they'll be back. It's only a matter of time.

Finnish Lumber

When Rabbi Wein's yeshiva, Shaarei Torah, was being built, one of the students' parents, who was in the building trades, called Rabbi Wein with good news:

"Rabbi, I think I can purchase for you, at cost, some of the finest structural timbers. They are imported from Finland and are guaranteed to last over 150 years. This timber costs a little more, than the domestic lumber we have on order but native wood will begin to decay after 90 years. I think it's worthwhile."

Rabbi Wein listened to the offer and thanked him for his enterprise but turned him down. "Douglas fir will be good enough for our yeshiva high school," he explained. "In America we build too well and we build for too long. Things move so fast it's hard to make calculations for 200 years from now.

"In this country, people move very quickly. The average length of a mortgage in the United States is seven years. Permanence interferes with a good time. It's no fun having to take care of an old place. It's 'neater' to rip it down and start all over again.

"Every *golus* has presented problems to Jews. The *golus* in America is a very shaky one despite the many assurances to the contrary. We think we are so successful that we can transcend the immorality that surrounds us. Don't you believe that! We need to be ready to move. We don't need wood that will outlast our grandchildren's great grandchildren. Historically, there are very few Jewish buildings which remain in Jewish hands after 90 years."

Rights of First Refusal

Rabbi Wein's father-in-law, Rabbi Eliezer Levine, *zt'l*, had been the Rabbi of a synagogue in Detroit for forty-five years. When Rabbi Levine started out, the biggest synagogue in town was a Conservative one with one of the largest memberships in America. Fifteen years later, when Detroit's middle-class population began to move to the suburbs, the congregation sold its synagogue to an upscale Baptist church and built a magnificent structure on the outskirts of the city.

Twenty years after the first migration, the congregation felt the need to relocate again, and bought property in the adjoining suburb. They sold their old edifice to the same Baptist group which had bought their original synagogue in central Detroit.

At the closing everything went smoothly, as the lawyers expedited the second sale of a synagogue building to the church. The representatives of the church even asked for the rights of first refusal when the Jews decided to sell their next building. They also inquired if they could be consulted by the building committee of the synagogue to provide design input for the new building. The Baptists knew how to plan ahead.

Golus in America

Shopping in supermarkets gives Rabbi Wein an opportunity to see what's going on in the wide world of Monsey. He likes to go about his business as discreetly as possible but people insist on blowing his cover. It must be disconcerting for those who know him to see him queuing up at the checkout counter.

"Rabbi Wein, what are you doing here?" the question is asked.

His answer is equally direct, "Where else should I shop?"

"A Rabbi shopping for food?" is the second most popular query.

He answers, "Rebbitzins need food to cook, too."

He really doesn't like to shop, so he doesn't make small talk; "When the going gets tough my answers are short but not curt. I'll do almost anything to get out of the supermarket." he reveals.

Most of the time no one notices him as he goes about his business quietly, observing the passing parade. "I watch the religious Jews and the not-so-religious. On Passover, for instance, I see people who buy a pound box of *matzah* and pack it along with their bacon and sausage, and I think to myself, 'How many more pounds of sausage before that bag won't have any *matzah* at all? Next Pesach? Six more Pesachs?' Half the Jewish world is singing, 'LeShona habah b'Yerushalaim' (Next year in Jerusalem) and half are singing 'More Park Sausages, Ma . . . .'

"More than anything, what I'm really looking for is my *Shabbos* speech," he reveals. "That special incident which can help focus on the task of becoming a good Jew."

He provides a couple of examples. The first happened in the bottle redemption center at our local supermarket.

❦ ❦ ❦

On one grocery shopping trip Rabbi Wein noticed a ruckus taking place at the bottle redemption center. An employee was harassing a nine-year-old boy dressed in Chassidic clothes. His *payos* were wrapped around his ears, his *tzitzis* hung loosely out of his shirt and his European-styled velvet cap was perched precariously on the back of his head. The argument pivoted on a nickel bottle.

The boy was insisting that he had brought nineteen bottles and was entitled to 95 cents in redemption money. The attendant, a young man around eighteen and about twice the size of the young Jewish boy, disputed the count. He insisted that one of the bottles was not acceptable. The hair on his head was scalped round about his skull an inch above his ears but the remaining hair on top tended to fly around when he got agitated. "You got this one from home delivery or something. We can't credit you for it."

The Jewish lad demanded the credit. "Look, I brought in eighteen good ones and the nineteenth is good too. I need that nickel."

"We need a lot of things, but you ain't getting it. It's no good and that's that."

"I'm going to talk to the manager." The young boy whirled around and left the confrontation, walking away with a self-important air. His opponent didn't pay attention to the threat. Turning his back on the boy he went about his bottle sorting tasks. In effect, the argument was over.

The boy realized that Rabbi Wein had been witness to the argument and as he walked by him, he shrugged his shoulders in mild disappointment and said: "I should go to the manager, you know, but what can you do?" Before he skipped away, he winked at Rabbi Wein conspiratorially and added, "That's *golus* for you."

Our *golus* is the sweetest, most self-conscious, and seductive *golus* we ever experienced. Consequently, it is the most perplexing in our history.

※ ※ ※

The other story happened in the same store.

It was evident that the couple in front of Rabbi Wein was foreign to our culture. Their clothes reminded him of America in 1950. The woman wore a rayon flowered-print dress and her companion a dark polyester suit with a very wide tie. They walked slowly without a shopping cart, marveling at the display of food.

They looked like recent arrivals from Eastern Europe and were stupefied by the variety of food choices that were offered. In a state of deep emotion, they hung on to each other like kids in a toy shop, pointing and exclaiming.

Rabbi Wein found their excursion interesting to behold so he followed them up the "macaroni section" and out into the aisles reserved for pet food.

When they got to the dog food they stopped cold in their tracks. Staring at the fifty-pound bags of dog food, they lost their bearings completely. Pointing at the sacks of pet food they turned to Rabbi Wein, the nearest bystander, and asked wonderingly, 'You have special food for animals?'

"Yes," he told them, "we call such food, pet food. We feed it to our cats and dogs."

"In Russia," the man said, "we bought this food to eat many times."

"They shrugged their shoulders and shuffled away, upset that Americans could feed dogs and cats with food that Russia fed to the general populace."

> "Thus we gain perspective on a shopping trip," Rabbi Wein concludes. "We learn from awe-struck immigrants and a child that we are in golus but we could be in worse places. I don't know if I ever found the appropriate Bible chapter for these events, but if I'm ever stuck I can always go back to the supermarket to shop for more stories."

The Jewish Problem

A woman once complained to Rabbi Wein that he had not advised her son properly when he consulted him about the possibility of going to medical school. The young man was torn between staying in yeshiva and moving on into the "real world." Rabbi Wein's statement that "even if one does leave the yeshiva, he should never leave early and he should never leave happily," struck a chord inside him. He decided to continue learning and eventually joined the *semichah* (rabbinic ordination) program.

"How could you do this to my son?" the woman wanted to know. "Rabbi, what if he is to be the one to discover the cure for cancer and now you've prevented that. Do you want that on your conscience?"

Rabbi Wein answered with a story: Once a man from a small town, of around 300 people including around 150 Jews, sent his son to university in Berlin. They were quite proud of him since he was the first young man from their small shtetl to go off to university. When the first semester had ended and the student returned home for his vacation his father was very excited to see him and find out how life was in the big city.

"Nu," he said, "tell me about the Jewish community."

"*Tatte*," the boy said, "there are over 300,000 Jews in Berlin."

"300,000!" cried the father. "What a *kehillah* (community)! And tell me, how many *goyim* are there in Berlin?"

"Three million," answered the son.

"Three million?!" The father was puzzled. "What do they need so many *goyim* for?"

"The Almighty also created non-Jews," Rabbi Wein told the disheartened mother. "Where is it written that the cure for cancer must be discovered by a Jew? Let a Chinese or African doctor find it. Let that be the world's problem. But Jewish problems can only be solved by Jews. If a young man has the opportunity to work for the Jewish people he should jump at it because he is the only one who can do it.

"When Elisha the Prophet was asked to help the poor widow, he told her to get all the jugs, pitchers, and vessels that she could; bring anything you can find, he told her. She did so and he poured the miraculous oil from his jar filling all her receptacles. But when there were no more barrels to fill, that was it. The oil stopped. Had she found more, she would have had more oil. Elisha's supply of oil was unlimited.

"The same is true of the Jewish people. The Torah is our oil, and it is unlimited. What the Jewish people need is more receptacles to take in the oil and pass it on to all those who have been lost through assimilation and the other plagues that the *golus* brings upon us."

Polarization

Once, Rabbi Wein was speaking to a group of business people who belonged to a Reform Temple in Little Rock, Arkansas. After his lecture, a visitor from an adjoining city approached him and bemoaned the fact that the branches of Judaism were growing further and further apart.

"I don't know if we can move closer together—you guys (Orthodox) don't give an inch. In order to survive, we've got to adjust to the times—we've got to have a dialogue about this."

Dialogues have a way of becoming debates and Rabbi Wein knows that no one wins debates; instead he offered him a story:

"There's a legend that is told about the Baal Shem Tov. Once this saintly man had a *golem* (an artificial human being endowed with life), which did all the menial work around his house and was only too happy to do it because he was made for that purpose. However, the *golem* could only do one task at a time. If he was given more than one thing to do he wouldn't do anything right.

"In preparing for a long, important trip, the Baal Shem Tov sent the *golem* outside to get the wagon ready for the road. In the excitement of preparing for the trip he told the creature to grease the wagon and to secure the traveling trunks. The *golem* rushed into the barn to collect the grease can and the heavy twine. When he got to the wagon, he was so happy to be given these tasks that he fell to his work with abandon. In his enthusiasm, he liberally applied grease to the wheels and the axles. But when he saw there was grease left in the can, he smeared it over the entire vehicle, seats and all. If greasing four wheels was so good, he thought, greasing everything would be so much better. The *golem* just couldn't be given too much to do.

"When it came to tying down the trunks, the *golem* had made such a mess that he slid all over the place. There was no way to stabilize himself long enough to fasten the trunks to the wagon. When the Baal Shem Tov and his entourage started to mount the wagon they, too, slid around looking for a dry spot to grasp. Everyone had to get towels to wipe away the grease before the trip could begin.

"Orthodox Judaism is like that wagon. It's rickety and old-fashioned and people think that it's too old to make the trip. But the wagon was built so well that it gets us to where we're going. When we start to fiddle with it and change the traditional way of doing things it gets so slippery that sometimes we slide all the way out of the wagon."

Pluralism

"When I was the Rav in Miami Beach," Rabbi Wein recalls, "the Reform Temple was across the street. I befriended the Rabbi there and over the years we found we could be helpful to one another. There were always some public matters that concerned the whole Jewish community, issues that both of us could support, so I maintained contact with him. In fact, we became so friendly that after a while we used to learn together on a regular basis. (I promised him that if he didn't tell, I wouldn't tell either.)

"One Passover he called me up and asked for a favor, 'My son is just back from Brown University and he is home for Passover. But he doesn't want to sit with us. He wants to attend a real Seder. Therefore, I'd like for him to be your guest.'

" 'Of course,' I said. 'Send him over. Jackie and I will be pleased to have him.'

"So the young man came and spent the first night of Pesach with my family. He had a good time. In fact the Seder service had such an effect on him that he told his father that he wanted to change his major in college. He no longer wanted to study law; now he wanted to go to Hebrew Union College and became a Rabbi, a reform Rabbi. And that's what he became.

"I always thought the problem was that he didn't attend the second Seder. Maybe then he would have become Orthodox."

❦ ❦ ❦

Franz Rozenzweig, the great Jewish philosopher, in the preface to his memoir, *Star of Redemption,* mentions that he was engaged to a Roman Catholic girl. He was in the process of converting to Roman Catholicism when World War I broke out. He was a captain in the German Army when, in 1914, Germany invaded Eastern Europe. Initially the campaign was very successful and the Germans occupied huge sections of Poland where a large religious Jewish population lived. Rosenzweig had never before come into contact with religious Jews.

He writes that for the first time in his life he went to a synagogue to attend services on *Kol Nidre* night (Yom Kippur). He describes that night and the effect the synagogue services had on him. He didn't understand one word of the service but it had such a profound effect on him that it changed his whole life. He wrote back to his fiancee that he was not going to marry her. That single experience spurred him into becoming an observant Jew. He studied Judaism and after the war, embarked on his career as a Jewish philosopher.

Jewish experience is the basis for building Jewish people. It's a simple idea but a powerful one nevertheless.

Esrog and Lulav

A call came to Rabbi Wein from a Reform Rabbi in Ohio.

"I got your name from my father who used to work with you when you were a lawyer in Chicago. He said you might be able to help me out. I have a problem.

"I'm a new rabbi here and I'm a bit more traditional than the previous rabbis of this congregation, so there's a conflict. This year, for *Succos*, I would like to have a *lulav* and *esrog* brought into the synagogue. I feel that the symbols of the holiday should be there in the temple for the congregants to see and hold."

He explained the problem further, "Since these are symbols of traditional observances, the Temple Ritual Committee must approve their inclusion. The committee met a week before *Yom Kippur* and decided that the *lulav* and *esrog* don't belong in our synagogue. This is the way they phrased it, 'For eighty years we haven't had a *lulav* and *esrog* and that's our tradition. We don't want to break with tradition.'

The young Rabbi went on, "we've got a number of young people in the synagogue and we're going to do it anyway. We ordered fifteen sets of *lulav* and *esrog*. But we examined the calendar and realized that this year the first day of the holiday of *Succos* falls on a *Shabbat*. Reform Jews don't observe a second day of *Succos* and since we're not allowed to carry an *esrog* and *lulav* to synagogue on *Shabbat*, we're in a quandary."

To complicate matters, he related that the members of the Ritual Committee went to the Orthodox Rabbi in town and got a letter from him stating that the Orthodox synagogue won't have a *lulav* and *esrog* in synagogue on *Shabbat* because it's not permitted. So they came to their young Rabbi with this letter and said, "We can't have a *lulav* and *esrog*; the Orthodox aren't going to have these symbols in their synagogue on the first day of *Succos*. So we're not going to have them either. After all," they said, "we can't be more religious than the Pope."

"Rabbi Wein," the caller asked, "what should we do? We know it's *Shabbos*, but we'd like to bring the *esrog* and the *lulav* with us on *Succos*. We think it would make a big difference to us in celebrating the holiday."

The unorthodox question caught Rabbi Wein off guard. He shifted the burden back to the Reform Rabbi. "Before I give you my answer. Tell me, what would you like to do?"

The Reform Rabbi paused and then said, "I've thought a lot about this and I'll give you an answer which has some Talmudic reasoning to it. Here's the logic: the Orthodox have *Shabbat*, so on the first day of Succos they can get along without the *lulav* and *esrog*. We in the Reform Temples don't even have *Shabbat*, therefore, we can't afford not to have the *lulav* and *esrog*. We must take them into the synagogue on *Shabbat Succos*."

Rabbi Wein brightened. "Son, I couldn't have said it any better."

> Rabbi Wein concluded: "What has happened to a great deal of our people is not that they don't observe. Rather, the religion is not theirs any longer. They don't have the holidays or the zemiros, not the rituals, and not the tears and certainly not the joy. The lulav and esrog are gone and, sad beyond words, they know they don't have it. Some return because they'd like to be a part of it. Some don't know how to return. Some speak out, but most remain silent. When Esau didn't receive the blessing from his father, Isaac, he gave a great shout,

"Where's my blessing?" Even Esau knew he had nothing. A great many Jews have awakened to the fact that they have nothing, too."

Yuppie Wein

When he graduated law school, Rabbi Wein was hired by a law firm as a junior associate. He describes his first day on the job:

"Just like any ambitious Jewish boy I was eager to make good and volunteered to go anywhere and take on any kind of task. The senior members of the firm took me at my word and on my very first day sent me all over Chicago to take testimony from witnesses in a negligence case we were litigating.

"The day was fatiguing but I felt I had accomplished a lot. I had secured crucial testimony in a very professional manner; I wrote affidavits and had them witnessed and notarized and was feeling pretty good about myself. I returned to the office later that night and logged in my time and activities in the journal we were instructed to keep. Around eight o'clock, long after it had become dark, I realized that I had missed *minchah* (afternoon prayers)."

He thought to himself, "If that's the first day on the job, what's going to happen when I get real pressure? I wonder what else I won't pay attention to? I decided then and there to build my day around my spiritual needs and not fit them in haphazardly."

He reminds his students, "It can be done as long as priorities are in the right order."

Golus Shorts

A Rabbi in yeshiva once told young Berel Wein that his generation was supported by two things: "*maftir* and *niftar*." If it weren't for *bar-mitzvahs* and *yahrzeits*, the synagogues in the thirties and the forties would have been empty.

※ ※ ※

According to Rabbi Wein: "To the European Jew, God was part of the family. We, alas, don't have that perception. We outsmarted ourselves and became very modern, modern orthodox, modern conservative, modern modern . . . "

※ ※ ※

When Rabbi Eliyahu Mayer Bloch founded the Telshe Yeshiva in 1941 in Cleveland, he went to the bookseller and ordered a *Kitzos HaChoshen*, a famous seminal work in Talmudic jurisprudence. It was a basic text in all European yeshivos. The bookseller said, "Here, I have one copy left." He dusted it off and handed it to the Rabbi. "Take care of this book. It is the last *Kitzos* that will ever be sold in America."

Rabbi Bloch who had come to rebuild Torah in America, was furious. He retorted, "I guarantee you that more copies of the *Kitzos* will be published to be sold in America than ever before in history." Time would prove him right.

> "We are living in great times, but we are a small generation. Other generations had people who could have handled our problems. Now, in the last fifty years the Almighty has piled such problems on us that it would take great leaders to help us. But this mismatch is the way God wants it! We don't have

men with the drive and vision of Reb Eliyahu Mayer so we must rise to the challenge."

Four Wise Men

Driving in a car, headed for an important rabbinical meeting, were the following dignitaries: a famous Jewish publisher, a famous doctor, a renowned *Rosh Yeshiva* (Yeshiva Dean), and that famous traveler, Rabbi Berel Wein.

The four were discussing the vast changes that religious life in America has undergone from the time they were children. Then, almost everyone went to public school. Religious education was conducted as an extracurricular activity. Rabbi Wein was quick to point out that elementary schools in the forties had separate entrances for the boys and girls.

Still, they all agreed that the neighborhood public school was not the ideal environment for Orthodox youth. They remembered how the Christian holidays were celebrated with elaborate assembly programs. Even the everyday curriculum emphasized holiday themes of the various Christian festivals. On Christmas, for instance, the teachers would choose stories with appropriate themes like "A Christmas Carol" by Charles Dickens or "The Gift of the Magi" by O'Henry.

With Rabbi Wein and the others marveling aloud how three public school kids could be on their way to the Agudah convention, the famous *Rosh Yeshiva* admitted, 'You know, I also went to public school.'

Without missing a beat, the doctor turned around in the front seat to face him, "Is that so?" he challenged, "Prove it. Let's hear you sing 'Silent Night!' "

The Rosh Yeshivah obliged them. Before he could get through the song the publisher joined in and they made the song sound "Jewishly soulful," according to Rabbi Wein, that noted listener.

Rabbi Wein's Grandfather

"In the early part of the century, my maternal grandfather, Rabbi Chaim Tzvi Rubinstein zt'l, was a Rav in Jerusalem. At that time, Israel was called Palestine and the country was ruled by Turkey." Thus, Rabbi Wein began his own story.

"He came to the United States in the middle of the First World War to raise money for the Jewish community of Jerusalem, which was starving to death under the Turkish rule and the British Embargo. Of all the possible fundraisers in Jerusalem at that time, Rabbi Rubinstein was the only rabbi with a Turkish passport. As a Turkish citizen, he was the only rabbi in Palestine who had the right to travel freely in and out of the country.

"Three months after he arrived in America, the United States entered the war to fight against the Central Powers, which included Turkey. As soon as war was declared, Turkish citizens who were visiting the United Sates on tourist visas were tracked down and arrested by the immigration authorities. In Chicago, my white-bearded *Zayde* (grandfather) was not hard to spot and he was quickly apprehended. He was detained in a small federal jail in Joliet County, Illinois.

"Word escaped the 'Big House' that a Rabbi was incarcerated there. When the Jews in the South Chicago community heard that a Yerushalmi Rav was in jail they became interested and decided to investigate. Sure enough, his credentials were impeccable and they felt that he was heaven sent. He would make an outstanding Rabbi for their community since there were ten thousand Jews in South Chicago and they had no Rav. On the next visitors day a committee arrived in prison to negotiate the conditions for his release.

"They explained the facts to him, 'There are ten thousand Jews in South Chicago and we have no one to learn with our children. We'd like to make a deal. In exchange for your agreement to serve as our Rav, we will obtain your release.'

"After Federal Prison, their offer looked appealing to my *Zayde* and he agreed to their terms. They contacted one of the Senators from Illinois to use his influence to have my *Zayde* released by the Federal Immigration Department. Shortly thereafter citizen Rubinstein walked out of jail almost a free man. He was still indentured to the community.

"After the war concluded, in 1919, he brought over the rest of the Rubinstein family, including my mother. That's how we came to Chicago. Who knows what would have happened had my *Zayde* been incarcerated in some other jail, say, Lubbock, Texas? I'd probably be talking with a Southwestern accent. Such is the destiny of the Jewish people."

❀ ❀ ❀

"My *Zayde* had a tremendous advantage over the rest of the world. He was an incurable optimist. In 1919, in the front room of his house, he opened the first Yeshiva in Chicago (what is today Bais Hamedresh LeTorah, the Skokie Yeshiva). Then it was the first yeshiva in the Midwest. My *Bubby* cooked, and the couple gave away their bedroom to serve as the dormitory for the boys. The first year, that's where the boys slept, all three of them, while *Bubby* and *Zayde* moved into the guest room.

"The day the yeshiva opened, a committee of synagogue members made an appearance to help my grandfather inaugurate the school. One of the leading *shomer Shabbos* congregants in Chicago came to wish him well. He was a very observant Jew and the unofficial leader of the traditional Jews on the South Side of Chicago.

"He wasn't being malicious, but he told my grandfather, 'Rabbi, I know you only have the best of intentions but it's not going to work out. Hair will grow on the palm of my hand before there will be a yeshiva in Chicago.'

"He didn't say this to cause my grandfather any harm. On the contrary, he wanted my grandfather to succeed. He merely thought he owed my *Zayde* his realistic appraisal. In the roaring 20's in America, he believed my *Zayde* was undertaking an impossible task. America was too modern, too secular, too demanding for the yeshiva life. It wasn't like Europe. Chicago was the bustling center of the most vibrant culture in the world. How could one concentrate on learning? America was one big swirling distraction. It was no place for a yeshiva.

"As a child, I remember wondering what those words meant —'hair on the palm of my hand.' The image disturbed me. My *Zayde* explained that it was only a figure of speech, but to this day I remember those words.

"When I tell the stories of my days growing up in Chicago my children think I'm making it up. They can't conceive of a world where yeshivas just did not exist. Public school now is anathema. The revival of yeshiva life in America since the war has been nothing short of remarkable. Hair may not have grown on the palm of that man's hand, but even he would agree that Yiddishkeit in this country is flourishing. Rabbi Chaim Tzvi Rubinstein's optimism was not misplaced. Thank God."

❦ ❦ ❦

"But we're not out of the woods yet."

"Now half of American Jewry is moving towards traditional expression of Yiddishkeit. The other half is in full flight, moving to the other extreme. There is no middle ground anymore.

"I remember Chicago the way it was. There were plenty of Jews in the middle; *Shabbos* Jews, *Yom Kippur* Jews, *Shas* Jews, *Tehillim* Jews. Jews of all kinds participating in a spirit of sharing and tolerance. When I was a little boy I sat on the porch of my *Zayde's* house on Douglas Boulevard. On *Rosh Hashannah* there were 40,000 Jews who walked to their local body of water and cast their sins away in the *Tashlich* ceremony. There wasn't a car that moved. Douglas Boulevard was black with people. In the Forties I remember that in the space of two square miles there were forty-two major synagogues with great rabbis in South Chicago alone. Hundreds of people prayed every *Shabbos*. Now we ask, 'What happened to all that?'

"Here in Monsey in 1991 we can't match those numbers. Even

in Flatbush, we can't get 40,000 people for *Tashlich*. In New City, Rockland County there are perhaps 20,000 Jews and except for the Reform temples there's no 'Yiddishkeit' whatsoever. Maybe there's one Lubavitch outpost, but for the rest of those New City Jews what is there in the way of traditional Judaism? Zero. All their grandparents went to *Tashlich*, and all their great grandparents were *shomer Shabbos*. What happened? It is mystifying.

"Here are some facts. In the world today there are approximately fifteen million Jews. Josephus writes in his *History* that in the time of the Destruction of the Second Temple there were about thirteen million Jews in the world. One out of every ten Roman citizens was Jewish; ten percent of the Roman Empire were Jews. In 2,000 years our numbers have not significantly increased.

"To put this in perspective, at the time of the Roman Empire there were about 30 million Chinese. Today there are over a billion and a half Chinese. Yet we Jews are still only fifteen million. No gain, flat; that is the price of *golus*.

"The losses in numbers is only part of the bill. In winter, even in suburban Orthodox Jewish communities you can't get a *minyan*; there's nobody to talk to. Even in 'Ihr HaKodesh,' the holy city of Monsey, you can't get people to come to a parlor meeting; you have to beg them to come.

"We are besieged by a society that stands against everything; a society that in three generations has all but obliterated Yiddishkeit from this country. This is a society that has produced phantoms of Jews hiding out and marrying out—eighty percent of whom have not visited Israel—Eighty-two percent have not given a dime to the U.J.A. We're not just talking about 'frumkeit.'

"In America we have produced Jews who are '7-11' convenience store Jews; who knows what would happen to them if serious pressures were applied? What would they be willing to do to preserve their lives? The country has built great fortresses against us; secularism, a society that is obsessed with things and not with people. This is a country where one-third of the population admits to mental illness. So the man who told my *Zayde*, 'Hair will grow on the palm of my hand before America will allow a yeshiva to be successful,' was more right than we care to admit. For the vast majority of American Jews he may have been on the money. Who needs it? Who wants it? In his mind, he was absolutely right!"

❦ ❦ ❦

"Where do we go from here? We cannot build a Jewish people through compromise and we cannot build a Jewish people without the Torah. Thank God, since the War we have witnessed a rebirth of Torah in this country. Everyone who was at the *siyum haShas* (celebration of the seven year cycle of completing the Talmud) in Madison Square Garden must marvel at the number of Jews there. The mere fact that such an event took place, forty-five years after the Holocaust is the major story. Nobody would have believed it. In the shadows of Buchenwald and Bergen-Belsen who would have had the courage to imagine such an event?

"In a generation when all the idols are bankrupted, when all the slogans have dissolved into nonsense, when all the myths have been shattered, then all that's left is a little Torah, the little spark of eternity in all of us.

"We live in a time of such turmoil that no one sees tomorrow. The Sages ask. 'How can a person save himself in such a time? Busy himself with Torah and good deeds,' is the answer. I often wonder why my grandfather told me those awful words spoken by his neighbor. I was only six or seven at the time but I continually think about that man and feel his words impressed me more than I knew. Many times when I wonder why I gave up the law to enter the rabbinate. I reflect on that man in Skokie and on his terrible words."

8

Rabbis and the Rabbinate

"Every synagogue gets the Rabbi it deserves."

The tone of a synogogue is a worthy issue to fight about."

Rabbis and the Rabbinate

abbi Wein grew up in Chicago. Around the corner from his house, his grandfather, Rabbi Chaim Zvi Rubinstein, lived with his wife, in a modest half of a two-flat dwelling. Every weekday on his way home from school, young Berel would stop off at his grandparents to learn a little Torah with his

grandfather. During his visits, he could count on listening to his grandparents discuss two major topics. One was the fate of the Jews in Europe and the other was whether their house would get painted in time for Passover.

Over the years, the elderly couple had managed to save $250 to do a complete painting of the interior of their house ($30 a room plus hallways and outside trim). As painting day drew near, the discussions inside the house intensified; the main questions were, "What color should we paint the hallways?" and, "Will the house be ready for *Pesach*?" Finally, the big day arrived and the painting crew was scheduled to come that evening to drop off their gear. Unfortunately, news of a different sort also arrived.

That day, early in Spring, the Rabbi received a letter from the *Vaad Hatzolah*, the organization trying to save European Jewry, that bore shocking news. He knew for some time that the Nazis were closing down Jewish institutions and confiscating Jewish property, but the letter revealed an ominous turn of events. The Germans were now tightening the noose and herding Polish and Lithuanian Jews into work camps and ghettos in Cracow and Warsaw were being walled in. The borders were sealed, and in the ghettos the Jews were beginning to starve. Finally, the letter stated that a new horror was taking place. It was reported that Jews in significant numbers were becoming so despondent, that for the first time in Jewish history they were committing suicide.

As the old Rabbi read this news it was as if the worst annals of Jewish history were being revisited, this time to the tempo of modern warfare. The Rabbi felt terrible and the paper shook in his hands. Young Berel, who was watching the old man read his letter, knew something was about to happen.

The Rabbi went to the phone and dialed the painter's number. His message was clear and to the point. "Hello, this is Rabbi Rubinstein. Please don't come to our house. We're not going to paint our house this year. Yes, that's right, that's right. We don't want it painted. Don't you worry about the money I'll take care of it . . . I'll take care of it."

When his wife heard him tell the painter not to come, she

demanded an explanation. Sadly, he handed her the letter he had been reading and informed her that European Jews were being made to starve.

"This is terrible. What's going to be?" she asked.

"Who knows?" he sighed, "who knows?"

She read the letter while the Rabbi went to the window and looked out at the traffic flowing by in the Chicago street. He intoned sadly, "I'm sorry but I canceled the painting; we'll get it done some other time." Then he turned around and addressed her in Yiddish, *"Ken men machen shein a haus ven yiden in der velt hoben azoi fiil yissurim?"* ("Can one make his house fancy when Jews are suffering so much?"). His sentence was formed by centuries of Jewish anguish; and only the Yiddish language could convey his feelings.

The Rebbitzen listened to his remarks, nodding silently. As an afterthought she asked, "But what about the painter's fee? What is going to happen to the money he expected to earn from painting our house."

Her husband responded, "I've already told him that he'll get his money anyway. It is too late to line up another job. We will pay him his $250 as if he did the job but we're not going to paint this house while Jews are suffering so much."

And so it was. The painter received his full compensation but for that *Yom Tov* and for the remainder of those horrid war years, the house continued to molder, flaking and unpainted to the end.

> *According to the Shulchan Aruch, when a Jew builds a new house or refurbishes an old one, an effort is made to leave a section of wall in the entranceway unfinished. This is to remind Jews of the destruction of the Temple. No more than fifteen people were present when Rabbi Wein told the above story on a weekday in Bais Torah Synagogue. We were learning precisely this halachah of leaving some part of a new construction unfinished. It was such a poignant story delivered in such*

a low keyed, offhanded manner that it astonished me.

After hearing the tale I felt Rabbi Wein's grandfather was related to me too, faintly, like a distant kinsman. All Jews have ancestors like Rabbi Wein's. And the summation of all our family stories form a grand saga, a national yichus sheet (genealogical records like family trees) containing events which have been burned for centuries into the hearts and minds of the great family of Jews called Am Yisroel, the people of Israel.

Rabbi Wein's Father-in-Law

For a half century, the spiritual leadership of Detroit, Michigan rested on the shoulders of one man, Rabbi Wein's father-in-law, Rabbi Eliezer Levin, zt'l. In a generation where Jewish leaders were scarce, Rabbi Levin stood out as a paragon of Torah and wisdom, guiding the Detroit community with strength and compassion.

Once, a congregant was marrying off a daughter and decided to deliver the wedding invitation personally to the Rabbi. Out of courtesy he asked when the Rabbi would like to be picked up to be brought to the hall.

"What time is the wedding supposed to start?" Rabbi Levin asked.

"*Kabbolas ponim* (a preliminary ceremony) is called for six and the *chuppah* (ceremony under the 'canopy,' i.e the actual wedding) for seven," was the answer.

Rabbi Levin thought for a moment and then asked that he be picked up in time to get there at six o'clock.

The father of the bride was very surprised. Usually when Rabbis asked him what time the wedding was supposed to start, they calculated it would start an hour later, i.e. 'Jewish time.' Not only did Rabbi Levin want to arrive on time, but he wanted to be there an hour earlier for *kabbolas ponim*!

When the day came, the Rabbi was picked up on time and delivered to the wedding hall at 6:00 P.M., almost beating the groom. The father of the bride wanted to know why the Rabbi appeared so early.

A friend of his explained, "Once there was a wedding in Detroit where neither family was financially well off. So the caterer, sensitive to the situation, cut every corner to keep costs down. The only problem was that the guests were late in arriving. The *chuppah* was delayed over an hour and by the time the feasting ended, the waiters were demanding overtime, which the caterer was forced to pay. Because of this added expense, the caterer's small profit evaporated. When Rabbi Levin heard of this, he took it upon himself to always be on time, for all celebrations, so that nobody should lose any money because of his inadvertant lateness."

Although Rabbi Levin had many more important things to do with his time than sit around at a wedding reception, his sensitivity to others was so acute that he would never be the cause of someone else's misfortune. That was one reason he was so cherished by the Jewish community of Detroit.

Shortest Speech Ever Made by a Rabbi

Rabbi Yisroel Salanter once found himself speaking to a restive congregation during the hiatus between *minchah* and *maariv*. By way of introducing the illustrious *mussar* master, the Rabbi of the synagogue got carried away and spoke longer than he intended. By the time Rabbi Salanter, the guest speaker, moved to the *bimah* (podium in the center of the synagogue), he sensed that his audience was not in the most receptive mood. He felt their patience had been exhausted and the speech he was about to deliver was superfluous.

Reb Yisroel simply said to them: "If only one Jew is moved, by only one word of my speech to pray *maariv* tonight with more *kavannah* (intensity of concentration); and even if it's only one word of the prayer; and even if that one Jew is just this speaker, then my speech would have been worthwhile." And he descended the *bimah*, opened his prayerbook and waited for the *chazan* to begin *maariv*.

Rabbi Meir's Back

Rabbi Wein attributes his Torah perspective to the European Rabbis who taught in the Chicago Yeshiva. They were veteran teachers who were rescued from the vanished world of Lithuania and Poland. However, they were strangers in a strange land.

Rabbi Wein remembers their predicament differently. "Everybody said the rabbis didn't speak English and the boys didn't speak Yiddish and it was a mismatch doomed to fail. But they were Jews, completed Jews, and it was a pleasure to be among them. They may not have been familiar with American culture but these men had been plucked from the flaming embers of European yeshivas for a reason. We, their American disciples, were that reason."

"Rabbi Yehuda Hanassi writes that he was able to compile the *Mishnah* because one day he was privileged to glimpse the back of Rabbi Meir, the legendary Sage, as he walked down a road. He didn't learn with the great man, he just saw his back. Had he seen his face, who knows what he might have accomplished? If American Jewry is going to amount to anything it's because we were taught by the remnants of the European rabbinate. We glimpsed the back of one thousand years of European Jewry. We have been living off their credit for two generations. They are drifting away from us and even their broad backs are disappearing. Who will carry us now? What will happen to us?

Frumkeit

According to Rabbi Wein, when he was a student in yeshiva in Chicago, "We were blessed with many outstanding Rabbis. They all were great scholars and one could learn much Torah from them. Some were such embodiments of Torah they were living *mussar* (ethics) lessons."

When he was seventeen, he attended a class delivered by a short, old, white-haired Rabbi who was almost totally blind. "Believe me," he recalled, "when I tell you he couldn't see very well behind those thick, cloudy glasses. He must have known the

Gemara (Talmud) by heart because he rarely looked at the pages. And as boys will be boys, even yeshiva boys, we took advantage of him every day. We had this Rabbi for two years and we had perfect, 100% attendance. No one was ever absent from his class — for two whole years! That's how poor his eyesight was. That must have set some kind of record for schools in the Chicago metropolitan area."

"On the other hand," says Rabbi Wein, "he was not completely defenseless. His saintliness was a powerful tool; it was irresistible. All of the boys felt he was a completely righteous man and they couldn't bear the prospect of disappointing him. The class learned the *Gemara* and *Tosafos* well and we were always prepared. The boys understood that he suffered when we didn't learn and we didn't want to cause him any pain. When he presented a problem in the *Gemara* someone always could provide an answer. If he would ask a question and we wouldn't know, we would be ashamed."

Just before Rosh Hashannah one year, the Rabbi mentioned that he needed a new hat for *Yom Tov*. Since Berel Wein was the only one with a driver's license, he offered to take his Rabbi to the hat store and bring him back to the yeshiva. "Buying a *frum* hat in those days in Chicago was no simple matter," Rabbi Wein explains. "Gentiles wore hats, too, and their hats were not so conservatively styled." The Rebbe consented to his pupil's offer.

On the way back, the Rebbe asked his student not to park the car in front of the yeshiva. He wanted to come into the school from the side. The yeshiva had two entrances — the main entrance was on Douglas but the Rebbe always used the one on Prospect. The boys thought that he didn't know the main entrance existed. Even if he did, he would never use it. Because of his poor vision, he could not find his way past the administrative offices to the classrooms. He had no problem with the Prospect entrance since it opened right into the classrooms.

Rabbi Wein remembered what happened next. "For some reason I didn't listen to him. Maybe because I didn't think it was important or because Prospect was a one-way street going the wrong way. I can't remember. Anyway, I pulled up to the yeshiva's main entrance, got out of the car and opened the door for him to disembark. He refused to move. I'll never forget the look on his face as he sat with his new hat box on his lap. I told him that the front door also led into the classroom part of the building, and I would help him with the box."

"He said he knew all about the main entrance, and then nudged me to get back into the car. 'I prefer the side entrance,' he said.

"Something about his refusal made me reflect on the layout of the yeshiva. What was so problematic for him? How could these offices be so forbidding? His words and the way he looked, a hint of color in his cheeks, made me realize the problem rested in the offices.

"The four secretaries with *shaitels* (wigs) must have been the problem. The boys considered them to be as ancient as mythology. These stolid citizens rarely moved beyond their desks. These must have been the people the Rabbi avoided. If he came in the entranceway on Douglas Street he ran the risk of 'seeing' the office personnel. Perhaps one of them would come out of the offices at the moment the Rebbe was passing . . . . This prospect loomed as a significant threat to his spiritual well-being. Now I knew why my Rebbe preferred the side entrance.

Rabbi Wein continued, "I got back into the car and drove around the block and parked on Prospect Street. He got out, shrugged off my offer to carry the hat and slowly walked in the side entrance. I watched him with reverence as he walked through the doorway of his choice, unsullied by his excursion into the wide, dangerous world."

Rabbi Wein uses this recollection as a springboard for his *mussar shmooze* (ethical improvement exhortation).

"In *Pirkei Avos* (2:5), Hillel says 'Do not believe in yourself until the day you die.' My Rebbe never wanted to test his *yetzer harah* (evil inclination) no matter how remote the temptation. He didn't want to assume anything about his virtue, even as he approached that stage of life when temptation loses its urgency. The *Gemara* relates that a certain *Kohen Gadol* (High Priest) during the Second Temple represented the Jewish people for many years. For decades he carried the sins of the nation with him on the awesome Days of Atonement. Time and again he encountered the *Shechinah* (Divine Presence) and he always emerged from the Holy of Holies unscathed.

"In his old age for some reason, this venerable, legendary man lost his faith. He stepped down and refused to conduct the service. He died shortly thereafter — an apostate. The Talmud instructs us to make fences around the Torah. My Rebbe built his modest fences and moved carefully through the world. In America we are apt to be careless about limits; after all, it is the Land of the Free.

"Our nearsighted Rebbe thought otherwise. He looked in front of him and saw minefields. He saw the way human beings really are — walking explosives, uncontrollable in their passions and intemperate in their dealings with others. What this Rebbe saw behind those cloudy lenses was the truth about the ways of the world. He needed to safeguard the living Torah that was his body and mind. He knew about the fate of other righteous individuals and he took nothing for granted. Taking a side door was a small price to pay to avert the fate of that *Kohen Gadol*."

Word of Mouth

When Rabbi Wein first came to New York many years ago he went to visit the famous *halachic* authority, Rav Henkin, who was then in his last year, and suffering from Alzheimer's disease. At one moment he could be carrying on a normal conversation and the next he would be completely incoherent. That is the tragedy of Alzheimer's. Sufferers lose control over many important functions, including speech. When the patient loses discretion over his behavior, people are witness to his baser self.

Some Alzheimer victims become explosively obscene, shouting curses at everyone or at no one and are so vituperative they must be gagged.

In his lifetime Rav Henkin had two major *halachic* disputes. One concerned the custom instituted in American yeshivas by Rav Aharon Kotler *zt'l* and others to recite *kiddush* and eat before *tekiyas shofar* (blowing the shofar) on *Rosh Hashanah*. Since the service on *Rosh Hashanah* inevitably lasts past midday, Rav Kotler was careful to eat before that time so people should not be fasting half a day on a *Yom Tov*. This became the accepted custom in much of the yeshiva world.

Rav Henkin strongly disagreed with this custom. He held that under no circumstances should the service be interrupted for *kiddush*. In his opinion the *mitzvah* of blowing *shofar* must be performed prior to eating anything. However, in deference to Rav Kotler, Rav Henkin did not publicly pursue the dispute.

The second dispute concerned the validity of marriages issued by non-Orthodox authorities. According to the decision of Rav Moshe Feinstein *zt'l*, a woman who was married under Reform auspices and later divorced without receiving a *halachic get* (divorce) was not obligated to obtain a *get* in order to remarry. Rav Feinstein determined that the Reform marriage was *halachically* invalid.

Again Rav Henkin disagreed and wrote that under no circumstances was the woman to be considered free to remarry and that the woman needed to find her first husband and obtain a *get* from him before marrying again. However, this time, too, Rav Henkin deferred to the opinion of Rav Feinstein, who was the acknowledged *posek hador* (Halachic authority).

Now, when Rabbi Wein, years later, came to speak with him, Rav Henkin was unable to talk coherently for any length of time. During their short interview the Rav drifted in and out of rational discourse. During the moments when the disease overpowered him he kept saying these same thoughts over and over: "No *kiddush* before *tekiyos*; she must receive a proper *get*. No *kiddush* before *tekiyos*; she must receive a proper *get*."

These interludes lasted a while and Rabbi Wein reports that, "I was very inspired by this revelation. He wasn't just repeating his position on *halachic* matters; that wasn't just Rav Henkin talking, this was the essential man. When a person loses control of his faculties, one gets to see what is beneath the surface; what the person really wants to say and who he really is."

Most people in the hospital for Alzheimer's babble about intensely private or relatively trivial matters, and some are so offensive that it is impossible to sit in the same room with them. Inside Rav Henkin were these two *halachos* that he had stifled for so long, and they were what came to the surface. As Rabbi Wein states: "Those who train themselves to develop clean tongues and clean minds will find themselves transformed into clean people."

Reb Yaakov

In Rabbi Wein's own words: "Anyone who knew Rabbi Yaakov Kamenetsky will know what I am talking about when I say he was the smartest Jew one could ever meet. He knew what made people tick and he thoroughly understood the ways of the world. He could size up situations in a wink.

"When things got rough for me, it was always comforting to know he was just a telephone call away. I remember his sound advice when I approached him with complex questions. I can hear his fearless epilogue even now, ' . . . and you can tell them that answer in my name. Don't be afraid, just say that you got that decision from me.'

"He was an old fashioned man who illuminated the modern world with his radiance. He always demonstrated great sensitivity to others. Once we drove the Kamenetskys to a wedding in Brooklyn. My wife, Jackie, sat in the back with his wife and I drove with him in front.

"When we got to the end of the Palisades Parkway, traffic slowed to a crawl before we could pay the toll to cross the George Washington Bridge. I got nervous because I knew they would delay the wedding until Reb Yaakov arrived. Waiting on lines did not then bring out the best in me, so by the time we got to the toll booth I was hardly civil. When it was finally my turn to pay the toll I couldn't wait to give the collector his three dollars and speed on my way.

"As I rushed ahead, Reb Yaakov noticed my indifference to the toll collector. He turned to me and said gently, 'You forgot to say 'tenk you.' It was his way of telling me, 'You may be in a hurry, but he's still a human being. One owes others something even in the most trivial exchanges.'

"The softest lesson often makes the deepest impression and I remember that lesson even today when they come over to my stopped car and begin to wash my windshield. Even when I can't wait to get out of there, I give them their quarters. Half out of fear, yes, but half because of Reb Yaakov, too. 'How would he respond?' I ask myself.

"Another time I heard that Reb Yaakov insisted that his driver not take the 'Exact Change' line. 'Go to the line with the toll taker, he needs a livelihood, too.' Reb Yaakov barely stood five feet tall but such was the stature of the man."

※ ※ ※

"Once, Reb Yaakov was accompanied by his son and granddaughter on an El-Al plane from Israel. It's a ten-hour trip and travelers can learn a great deal if they are in the right seats. In Reb Yaakov's row sat another senior citizen, Yerucham Meschel, the Head of Israel's Histadrut. (He didn't share Reb Yaakov's religious point of view.)

"During the course of the trip it became obvious that the granddaughter of Reb Yaakov doted on her *Zayde*. She couldn't wait to be of service to him. She constantly asked after his comfort, bringing him pillows and glasses of water. She did whatever she could to make her grandfather's trip pleasant. At the end of the trip the bejeweled neighbor remarked to Reb Yaakov that his own grandchildren didn't behave like that to him. 'Once they lay their hands on the toys I have brought for them, they ignore me. I can't understand your granddaughters behavior; she's so kind to you.'

"Reb Yaakov leaned over to him and said confidentially, 'It's really very simple. You have taught your children to be modern; you teach them to believe in evolution. They believe that apes were their ancestors, therefore, in their eyes, you are closer to the world of animals than they are. So why should they respect you? On the other hand, my granddaughter was brought up to believe that the first man, Adam, was made in the image of the Almighty, who is perfect. Unfortunately, since that time man had descended more and more. Every year he loses a little of that holy identity. My granddaughter treats her *Zayde* with respect because *Zayde* is closer to the first man, while she, my granddaughter, is closer to the apes.' "

The Smile of an Orphan

Mr. David Parzel, a relative of the Chofetz Chaim, told this story to the membership of Rabbi Wein's synagogue during an evening sponsored by the Sisterhood of Bais Torah. Mr. Parzel, who lived in a cottage right next to our synagogue, talked about his early life in the Chofetz Chaim's house in Radun.

One of the Chofetz Chaim's cousins had left the community to become a successful manufacturer in Estonia. In his quest for wealth, he had "freed" himself of the constraints of Orthodox observance. The *Haskalah* (secular enlightenment) was moving eastward. Even though the Baltic States were distant from the intellectual capitals of the continent, ideas have a way of spreading. The Chofetz Chaim saw that these ideas threatened Jewish survival.

One day tragic news reached him. He received a letter informing him that his non-observant cousin, Mr. Jacob Parzel, and his wife, had capsized in a sightseeing boat and drowned in the Baltic Sea off the coast of Scandinavia. Their only son, David, was attending school in Paris. No relative could be found who would take this eleven-year-old. The lawyer who wrote the Chofetz Chaim pleaded, "Surely, the great traditions of the Jewish religion recognize the plight of an orphan. It would be a great kindness if you would shelter this boy until we can find a suitable living arrangement."

Immediately the Rabbi wrote back: "Send David as soon as possible. Be assured that we are willing to prepare a home for him."

Within a month the boy arrived. Emotionally, the boy had survived the tragedy as well as could be expected. A clever student, he was totally ignorant of Jewish ritual and tradition. In the trunks which accompanied the lad were many books written in French, a whole library of classical music and a small violin. David said he loved music and wanted to continue to play his violin.

His wardrobe also created quite a stir in the Kagan household. His clothes were very modern. Turn of the century Parisiennes wore clothes that called attention to the wearer. The boy's fashionable attire clashed with the dull Lithuanian surroundings.

The young man wanted to fit in with the new family, so he allowed the Chofetz Chaim to change the way he dressed. He also agreed to learn religious subjects. However, there were certain things that the Chofetz Chaim was determined not to change.

Every Sunday morning a finely dressed man would arrive at the train station and the Chofetz Chaim would pick him up and take him to his house. After the man entered the Rabbi's house, the neighbors heard violins playing musical scales. They figured out that the Chofetz Chaim had hired a music teacher for the boy.

The townspeople wanted to know what was going on. Why did the Rabbi hire this man? What could the Rabbi be thinking? The music was nice, but it wasn't Jewish. Who knows what this music would lead to? They heard that the music teacher was also teaching the boy French subjects, including philosophy!

The Chofetz Chaim cleared the air. He delivered a lecture which referred to the rights of a Jewish slave who goes free after six years. At that time both "he and his children go free." In the Talmud, Rabbi Simeon asks, "Why does the Torah free the children; they were never enslaved?"

"We learn from this" the Talmud says, "that the master is bound to provide even the servant's children with food although they are not his slaves."

The Chofetz Chaim explained that the case of the children of a slave was similar to the orphan David. The boy was part of a family enslaved by an alien culture. The Chofetz Chaim took responsibility for the boy. In so doing, he obligated himself to provide the boy with his needs. As the master provided for the children of his slave, so too the great Rabbi took care of his ward. This poor orphan had other needs though. Only the Chofetz Chaim was sensitive enough to realize that.

"Can I do less for my cousin's son than what I am commanded to do for a son of a slave? I am obligated to have him continue in his customary education.

The Chofetz Chaim concluded, "Besides, my friends, the heart of an orphan is smiling, and so are the angels in heaven, so why are you disturbed?"

❦ ❦ ❦

The saintliness of the Chofetz Chaim was evident to all. Even gentile peasants who lived in Radun were impressed. As he rode through the countryside, they would beg him to stop and walk on their fields so their crops would be blessed.

David Parzel grew up in the Chofetz Chaim's house. He emigrated to America in his twenties and became successful in the publishing world. At the height of his career he was appointed one of the chief editors of the firm, Simon and Schuster. His niece, Carly Simon, carries on the musical traditions. In his eighty-sixth year he moved to a small carriage house on an estate next door to his relative Rabbi Gershon Zaks, the grandson of the Chofetz Chaim. He came full circle, living out the few remaining years of his life as close as possible to his spiritual ancestor, the Chofetz Chaim, Rabbi Israel Mayer Kagan.

Educational Planning

At the end of the summer semester, the Chofetz Chaim assembled his chief administrators and made plans to staff the yeshiva for the next semester. He described his plan for the faculty.

"Rabbi Zaks will take the lower class; Rabbi Faivelson will take the middle; Rabbi Gordon will work on fundraising; Rabbi Zissen is recuperating from a bad fall and can't teach till after the Holy Days; Reb Hirsh Levinson (the Chofetz Chaim's son-in-law) who was *niftar* (passed away) is studying now in *Gan Eden* (heaven) so he also needs coverage and Rabbi Kalmonowitcz will continue as *mashgiach*. That means we need three replacements right now."

As the Chofetz Chaim planned the yeshiva schedule, it became clear that he had perfect *emunah* (faith) in an afterlife. Rabbi Levinson was not lost, he was only working on a different assignment. For the Chofetz Chaim, *Gan Eden* was a place as real as Passaic, Teaneck, or Boro Park."

The Game of Marbles

When Rabbi Wein revealed to his guest, the Ponevezher Rav, Rabbi Yosef Kahaneman, that once he had applied for a Rabbinical position in his hometown, Chicago, and had been rejected, Rabbi Kahaneman shared this story with him.

When he began his career as a Rabbi, he left his hometown of Kula to search for a *shtele* (rabbinical position, leading a congregation). Years later, after successfully working as a rabbi in a few Polish cities, a position opened in his hometown. Rabbi Kahaneman eagerly wrote the selection committee in application for the post. They wrote him back a very polite letter of rejection. They wouldn't even give him a hearing. He couldn't understand it; he thought he had the inside track since he knew all the people on the committee.

He wrote again asking for clarification, suggesting they had made some error and had mistaken his application for someone else's. He waited for a reply but after a few weeks it became clear that they were not going to answer him. For whatever reason they didn't want him as their Rabbi.

Many years later at the height of his career he became Rav of Ponevezhe, a major center of European Judaism. One *Shabbos* he noticed one of the leading congregants from Kula in his synagogue. He had been a member of the hiring committee that rejected the Rav's application years earlier. Rav Kahaneman waited until *motzaei Shabbos*, then went over to his old townsman to ask him why the community had turned him down.

The man leveled with the now famous Rav, "My dear Rav, now you are famous and respected. You preside over a very large community. But you must understand that at the time you wanted the post in Kula, all we knew about you was from when you grew up in our town. We remembered you as a child playing marbles in our streets. It may sound unfair, but to us you always are that child. Nobody would have thought of you as the Rabbi, the leader, the one from whom we had to learn. Who in Kula would accept reproof from a marbles player?"

The Rabbi thanked him for his honesty. From there he continued to develop his career and reputation. After many successful years in Ponevezhe, he remarked that it was a good thing he hadn't grown up in Ponevezhe, "The children there played marbles in the streets, too."

Lo Sikom

The prohibition against taking revenge is one of the more difficult ones to avoid in a society that thinks as the great football coach Vince Lombardi did, "Don't get mad; get even." The Torah, however, sees things differently, to the extent that not only must one avoid getting back at those that offend, lo sikom, but one must also refrain from sending the offending party on a guilt trip, lo sitor. The great leaders of the Jewish people were fine examples of individuals with the ability to uphold these commandments. Rabbi Wein relates the following incident about Rabbi Abraham Isaac Kook who was the Chief Rabbi of Palestine prior to the establishment of the State of Israel and who was a great spiritual leader, outstanding in his mastery over his passions.

Rav Kook, when he was Chief Rabbi of Palestine had many detractors. His critics slandered him and hung posters criticizing his positions on matters of policy and religious observance. When he walked through the narrow streets of the Holy City, his enemies would even go so far as to empty their chamber pots on him. As Chief Rabbi, however, Rav Kook held onto certain indisputable powers that ruled the lives of his antagonists. For the society at large he was the supreme, official rabbinical authority in the country.

As God's marvelous sense of humor would have it, it once came to pass that one of Rav Kook's most rancorous opponents required a letter that had to be signed by none other than the Chief Rabbi himself. Too embarrassed to face Rav Kook directly, the man sent a messenger in his stead. The messenger went to the Rav's office and after pleading with Rav Kook to let bygones be bygones requested the Chief Rabbi write the official letter. Rav Kook sat down right away and wrote the letter. When he finished he put down the pen and gave the messenger the letter, but almost immediately asked for it back.

Rav Kook opened the letter and reread it word for word. He then gave it back to the messenger who left before Rav Kook could change his mind again. Rav Kook's assistant, puzzled by this, asked, "Why did the Rav want to see the letter he had just written?"

Rav Kook answered, "I reread the letter because I wanted to be certain that it did not appear to be written with any lack of enthusiasm. I wanted to make sure that subconsciously I did not hold back anything from this person."

The Nazir

Rav Kook was responsible for changing the lives of many people, but perhaps the person most affected by Rav Kook's dynamic personality and vast knowledge was his pupil, Rav David Cohen.

David Cohen, son of a Lithuanian Rav, was considered by many to be an *iluy* (a Torah prodigy) and demonstrated vast potential for Torah achievement. By the time he was sixteen, he rose to prodigious heights of Torah scholarship in the great yeshivas of Volozhin and Slobodka. Yet, at the age of eighteen he dropped it all. Defections from the yeshiva were not uncommon at the turn of the century and those who left, especially those with the enormous potential of a David Cohen, dealt a severe blow to the yeshiva world and the Torah community at large. "The yeshivas were hemorrhaging," observes Rabbi Wein. "They were losing their life-giving plasma."

David Cohen left for Germany, the bastion of culture and secular education in the western world. He attended the University of Heidelberg and the University of Freiberg where he happily found himself under the tutelage of a certain Professor Shapiro. Shapiro had once been a Rav who, like many of his students, abandoned tradition for the calling of a new "enlightened" way of life. He taught mathematics in Freiberg and attracted many former yeshiva students who chose him as an intellectual role model.

Their studies were not limited to mathematics. Often before class they would engage in deep Talmudic disputation, " . . . often without *yarmulkes*, on *Shabbos*, smoking cigarettes. They just loved to learn Talmud. It is hard for us to understand that frame of mind. We only associate 'learning' with the religious experience, while they learned purely for intellectual motives," Rabbi Wein observed in one of his taped "Biography" lectures.

Cohen received his Ph.D. in mathematics and went on to earn a second Doctorate in philosophy. At the age of twenty-six he joined the faculty at the University of Basel in Switzerland where he held chairs in both mathematics and philosophy. In 1914, Rav Kook was invited to speak at the founding convention of *Agudas Yisrael* in Austria. Almost as soon as he left *Eretz Yisrael*, World War I broke out. The Turks sealed the borders of the Holy Land making exit and entry into the country impossible. Rav Kook was effectively exiled from his country. It would be five years before he would be allowed to journey home.

For the first two of those years, he took up residence in Switzerland, accepting the position of Rav in a small hamlet named St. Gallan. In a chance meeting, Rav Kook was introduced to the young philosophy professor, Dr. David Cohen, and they spoke briefly. Cohen recalled later, that he was very attracted by the Rav's unique combination of scholarship and worldliness. A short while later, still enchanted by their first meeting, the professor called on Rav Kook. This time they spoke at length on all matters from philosophy to kabbalah, as David Cohen began to sense that he had found someone he could learn from, a mentor who could synthesize the old and the new. "He made me see that traditional Judaism often clarified modern philosophic trends and that the modern temperament clearly owed its intellectual heritage to classical Judaic ideas," Cohen recollects. After a sleepless night, Cohen heard Rav Kook recite the prelude to the *Parshas HaAkeidah* in the morning prayers. Something in his soul snapped; he had found his Rebbe.

When he had won Cohen's trust, Rav Kook challenged him, "Why are you making a fool of yourself? The university life is *sheker*, false, and if you stay here and get caught up in this career, you too will be *sheker*." It didn't take long for the professor to acknowledge the strength of the Rabbi's logic. In a very short period of time David Cohen transformed himself entirely. He became a *baal teshuvah* and for the rest of Rav Kook's stay in Switzerland he learned from him.

They both returned to Israel after the war and David Cohen took an oath of *nezirus* (to become a *nazir*) to atone for his previous behavior. As a *nazir*, he never cut his hair nor drank wine, and he continued so for the rest of his life. In the Torah world, he was known as "The *Nazir*" and was reputed to be a *tzaddik gamur* (a perfected individual).

In Rav Kook's eyes, his own temporary exile to Switzerland was engineered to save this one Jew. In fact, Rav Kook felt that the outbreak of the First World War occurred only to bring David Cohen back to observance. "*Hakol bishvil Yisroel*," everything exists for the service of the Jewish people. God will turn the world upside down to give one yeshiva dropout the chance to come home.

Like Father-in-Law Like Son-in-Law

Rav Kook was the son-in-law of the *Aderes* (Rabbi Eliyahu Dovid Rabinowits-Teumim) and he learned a great deal about practical rabbinics from his father-in-law. When Rav Kook assumed his first rabbinical position in the old Lithuanian *shtetl* of Zoimel, he was determined to keep the Jewish community there untainted by the influence of secularism that was sweeping the country. To do so he would have to create a sound moral infrastructure in the community and that called for strong leadership.

One of Rav Kook's first projects in Zoimel was to build a new *mikvah* (pool for ritual immersions). The old one was in a state of disrepair. Moreover, there were several *halachic* problems connected with its structure. Rav Kook knew that a *mikvah* was central to Jewish existence and had to be restored at all costs. This view was not shared by his congregants, who were not eager to finance the building of a new *mikvah*.

Rav Kook took the matter into his own hands. One Friday he came to synagogue about a half hour before *minchah* (afternoon prayers) and collected all the *talleisim* left on the benches in synagogue. In order to retrieve his *tallis* a synagogue member had to make a contribution, in cash, to the *mikvah* fund. It didn't take very long before the villagers of Zoimel had raised sufficient funds to rebuild their *mikvah*.

The Truth Consoles

Off the beaten track, on Old Nyack Turnpike in Monsey, lives an old and holy man, the Ribnitzer Rebbe. People come to him from all over the world to receive blessings in time of need.

There is no telling exactly how old he is now, but there are pictures of him that date back twenty years and he looks then to have been in his seventies. His body now looks withered and shrunken. But even today people sense this man is someone who lives on a different plane.

Not too long ago, one of Rabbi Wein's congregants went to the Rebbe to intercede for a friend who was seriously ill. After being ushered into a room he looked around but couldn't locate the Rebbe. He sat down at a table next to a chair with a *tallis* (prayer shawl) draped over it.

"Nu?" called out the Rabbi's assistant pointing at the chair next to him impatiently, "Nu?"

Only then did the visitor realize that he was seated next to the ancient *tzaddik*. The visitor peered around the *tallis* for a better view.

The Rebbe's face was bleached by age into a bluish whiteness. Once he had seen a snapshot of the Rebbe sitting in a throne-like chair. Then the Rabbi's features were sharply etched, his beard fiercely black and his bearing was serene and kingly. Now the frame was shrunken beyond belief and he was no longer erect.

"Write out the names on the piece of paper!" His helper suggested brusquely.

He wrote out the Hebrew name of his sick friend and placed it on the table. A blue-veined hand reached out and adjusted the paper. His assistant moved over to the Ribnitzer and read the names loudly, right by his ear. At that moment the old Rabbi's wife was hovering in the background. She called out to her husband that she knew the visitor was a fine person and came from an outstanding family.

The Rebbe looked at the names and remained silent for thirty seconds. He pushed the piece of paper away from him and in a thin, high pitched voice uttered some barely audible sounds.

"The Rabbi just gave your friend a *brachah* (blessing). He says she'll be all right for now," his assistant interjected.

The words, "for now" were ominously terse. What did he mean? The visitor was disappointed. He had hoped the Rebbe would say more, but the assistant ushered him out. However, after he got home he remarked to his wife that he felt strangely consoled.

He had been in the presence of a different kind of man. He felt this man had made a decision long ago to set himself apart and concentrate on important things. People came and drifted into his periphery but he was indifferent to them. He wasn't unfeeling, just removed.

The congregant concluded, "I had never met any one who cared less about the things of this world. He would have let me sit next to him unnoticed forever. It wasn't a matter of his being uncaring or inattentive. He was just content within himself. Although he didn't give me the reprieve I wanted, I felt he uttered the truth and that was consoling."

※ ※ ※

In a similar vein, Rabbi Wein relates an old story about a Chassidic Rebbe who was reputed to be a miracle worker. "In Poland," he says, "before the War the Rebbe would walk outside his synagogue to bless the new moon in the *kiddush levanah* ceremony. One moment before the congregation could begin the blessing, clouds floated across the nighttime sky and covered the moon. Since it is necessary to discern clearly the shape of the new moon during the ritual, all the praying stopped and the *minyan* looked at the Rebbe for orders. Without clarity they could not continue."

"Go inside," he said, "and get me a clean, white towel. Quickly, the attendant ran into the synagogue and a few seconds later returned with a small towel. The Rebbe took the towel and lifted it above his head. Then, in a strange, slow, wiping motion he waved at the clouds. The whole synagogue craned their heads heavenward. No one said a word as the Rebbe cleaned the sky!"

"Slowly, the clouds began to drift by and the moon revealed itself, a sickle of pristine, shimmering whiteness. The men finished praying and joined hands in a spirited circle of dancing. Even the attendant who accompanied the Rebbe everywhere and had seen a lot of wondrous events in his time was impressed. He sidled up to the Rebbe and confided that even for the Rebbe that was a formidable trick.

"The Rebbe looked at the white towel in the beadle's pocket and explained, 'My father could do this without a towel.' "

> *The sick woman of "The Truth Consoles" died of her illness later that year. However, she did live long enough to be present at her youngest daughter's wedding and see her first grandchild born. "For Now" had been defined. Undoubtedly, the Ribnitzer Rebbe has great powers, but Rabbi Wein is fond of quoting the memorable warning of the Lithuanian Rabbis: "You shouldn't argue too strenuously with destiny." (Du zols nisht upraysen mit der hashgacha.)*

A Grobbe Taus

Never trust the academic scholars;
they see the trees
but they miss the forest.

Rabbi Wein was doing research on the development of the great Chassidic dynasties in the Eighteenth and Nineteenth centuries and he came across a wonderful book on the period. The author had labored mightily and produced a voluminously annotated tome on the very subject the Rabbi needed. It was a marvelous piece of scholarship, thorough and discerning, running over four hundred pages. But although it was scrupulously researched, on one issue it missed entirely.

The scholar reported that the Gerer Rebbe, Rabbi Avraham Mordechai Alter was once asked how many Chassidim he counted in his domain. The Rebbe decided to have a little fun with the interviewer and framed his answer impishly. *"Ich vais nisht vi fill, ober ich gloib az iber tzen tousand essin Yom Kippur."* ("I don't know how many followers I have, but I believe that ten thousand eat on Yom Kippur.") He answered indirectly because he didn't want to reveal the exact population of his flock. He meant that there were at least ten thousand children, those too young to fast on Yom Kippur.

The author of the study concluded, "This statement of the venerable Rabbi was compelling evidence to indicate that religious observance was on the decline even in the bastions of Orthodox Jewry. If the followers of the Gerer Rabbi ate on Yom Kippur, imagine what the secular Jews were doing."

Sometimes the scientists mistake facts for truths.

Sayings of the Kotzker

The Kotzker Rebbe, Rabbi Menachem Mendel Morgenstern (1787-1859) was famous for his sharp wit and uncompromising search for the truth. Woe to the adversary who stood in his way. He was master of the caustic aphorism, as a small sampling will attest:

❧ ❧ ❧

"Better a *rosha* (evil persom) who knows he's a *rosha* than a *tzaddik* (righteous man) who knows he's a *tzaddik*."

❧ ❧

When the Kotzker was asked: "Where does one find God?" he replied, "Wherever you let Him in."

❧ ❧ ❧

Chassid: "Rabbi, What should I do? I've gone through *Shas* (the entire Talmud) six times."
Kotzker: "Yes, but how much of the *shas* has gone through you?"

❧ ❧ ❧

The day before *Rosh Hashannah*, a prospective *shofar* blower was bedeviling the Kotzker with questions: "What deep, mystical thoughts should I have in mind when I blow the shofar?" The Kotzker pointed to the *machzor* (prayerbook) and implored him to keep his focus on two letters: *shin* and *beis* (S,B). The *shofar* blower begged the Kotzker to tell him what those mystical letters meant. The Kotzker simply said, "*shoitah blozst, shoitah blozst!*" (Fool blow! Fool blow!)

❊ ❊ ❊

The realistic Kotzker Rav used to say: "The Messiah can come anytime he wants to; it's up to him because spiritually things are not going to get much better." (He said this in the middle of the 1800's, when saintly giants still walked the streets of European ghettos.)

❊ ❊ ❊

The Kotzker's insights into psychology of everyday behavior have a modern cast to them and seem to predate by a hundred and fifty years the neo-Freudian world of interpersonal psychology: "If I am and you are, because I am myself and you are yourself, then I am I and you are you; but if I am I because you are you and you are you because I am I, then I am not I, and you are not you."

❊ ❊ ❊

"Is it possible to bring the dead back to life? Still better, is it possible to bring the living back to life?"

❊ ❊ ❊

"All that is thought should not be said, all that is said should not be written, all that is written should not be published, all that is published should not be read."

❊ ❊ ❊

" 'Thou shalt not steal' means thou shalt not steal from yourself — do not deceive yourself."

A Good Memory

The Rogotchover Gaon, Rabbi Yosef Rosen was known to have a phenomenal mind and a photographic memory. His fellow townsman, Rabbi Meir Simcha HaKohen of Dvinsk used to describe the mental prowess of the Rogatchover as something greater than a fabulous sense of recall: "The world makes a mistake," said Reb Meir Simcha. "He doesn't have a good memory; I have a good memory. I can remember a page I haven't seen in twenty years. It is difficult for me to forget anything. But the Rogatchover doesn't have to remember. He constantly learns and reviews the entire Talmud every month, twelve months a year! That's not memory — that's like remembering what your address is or your birthdate or the name of your dearest friend. We memorize, he just learned it!"

The Revenge on the Tzaddik

The Talmud states that one who pretends to be poverty-stricken in order to collect charity is punished by actually becoming poor. The same is true of the person who gains sympathy from others by pretending to be a cripple. He will become crippled before he dies.

After teaching this to his students, the Chasam Sofer, Rabbi Moshe Sofer was asked, "What will happen to the person who pretends to be a *tzaddik* (a righteous individual)? Perhaps he will become a *tzaddik*?

"No," the Chasam Sofer replied sadly. "He won't leave this world until, unfortuunately, he believes that he is a *tzaddik*."

When the Chasam Sofer was appointed Rav of Pressburg, parts of the Jewish community were controlled by the *maskillim* (anti-religious) Jews. As soon as he arrived in the city, he called a meeting of all Jewish leaders. He felt the Jews needed to form a unified political group to represent their interests to the non-Jewish world.

At the meeting, the *maskillim* scoffed as his efforts and derided the traditional community. In mocking tones, the leader of the *maskillim* flaunted his irreligiosity before the Chasam Sofer. "I have committed every *avairah* (sin) mentioned in the Torah. And the Lord has seen fit to ignore my sins. What do you say about that?"

"I am afraid you are mistaken. You have transgressed all *aveiros* except one," the Chasam Sofer gently corrected him. "If you had committed suicide, then you would have been perfect."

The Satmar Rav and the Butcher

When Rabbi Wein began his career as the Rav in Miami Beach the Satmar Rav, Rabbi Yoel Teitelbaum, was one of his first visitors. Rabbi Yoel told him a story that happened when he, too, was starting out as a Rabbi in his first job.

When the Satmar Rav was twenty-two he took his first position in a city on the Hungarian-Roumanian border. It was customary in European communities for all the *shochtim* (butchers) to convene at the house of a new Rav at the end of the first month of his tenure and turn over their slaughtering knives to him. This symbolized that the butchers were submitting themselves to his authority. Then the Rabbi would examine the knives and if they were kosher, return them.

Fourteen *shochtim* assembled and thirteen of them gave the Rav their knives to examine. The fourteenth *shochet* was a grizzled veteran of many years. He waited until the others left and then he approached the Rav's table and put his foot up on a chair. He raised his kaftan and showed the Rav his *chalif* (knife); it was stuck way down into his boot.

"For forty years I have reviewed the laws of *shechitah* every thirty days," he started, "and every day I went to work and certified to myself that this knife has a kosher edge. You've been here for thirty days, Rabbi Teitelbaum . . .," and he pointed to the Torah scroll in the ark. "Now, if we take out a *sefer* Torah, (Torah scroll) are you equipped to answer, on the spot, that this *sefer* Torah is also without blemish?" The novice Rabbi did not utter a word so the old *shochet* walked out of the study — his knife still sheathed in his boot.

The Satmar Rav admitted to himself that he had not reviewed the *halachohs* of Torah scrolls. That night he decided to refresh his knowledge of the *halachos*. Fortified by his exhaustive review, he walked into the synagogue later that week, opened the ark, drew out the first of that synagogue's scroll and began to inspect the parchment letter by letter.

The following *Shabbos*, during the Torah reading, the reader stopped and pointed to a questionable letter in a word. (The Torah must be perfectly transcribed. Any seriously cracked or misshapen letter can invalidate an entire Torah scroll.) The new Rabbi was able to resolve the question on the letter quickly and authoritatively. His performance so impressed the venerable *shochet* that before long he reappeared before the Satmar Rav to present himself and his knife to the new Rav and conceded, "I see your devotion to Torah is as sharp as my knife; I would be honored to submit my knife to you for inspection."

The Rav accepted the knife from him and scrutinized it carefully before returning it to the *shochet*. Rabbi Teitelbaum told Rabbi Wein, "I didn't give it back to him too fast. I didn't want him to feel that just because he thinks I'm good, it doesn't mean that, automatically, I think he's good."

❦ ❦ ❦

When he left the legal profession after spending nine years practicing law in Chicago, Rabbi Wein confesses he missed the stimulation of the "Big City." However, ministering to congregants in a synagogue in Miami Beach had its advantages. "My home and my synagogue were visited by some of the luminaries of the Jewish world, especially during the cold winter weather."

One winter he again welcomed the Satmar Rav and a group of his followers into his home and into his synagogue. "My synagogue was the only one then located in the area where he was staying that winter." Rabbi Wein explains.

During the Rebbe's visit, Rabbi Wein was afforded the opportunity of getting to know the great leader on a personal basis. It was not too long before he discovered the Rebbe possessed a quick sense of humor. The Rebbe was always accompanied by a group of his followers. One of them came across an account in a local newspaper of the search for the *kever* (burial crypt) of Shmuel HaNavi (Samuel the Prophet). At the time, there was some doubt that the tourist attraction in Nebi Samual reputed to be the *kever* of Shmuel HaNavi was really his burial place. The tour guides said it was, but some scholars were unsure. The Chassid chortled that the archeologists didn't know very much, "How can they know where Shmuel HaNavi was really buried? Those Israeli experts don't know anything!"

The Satmar Rebbe didn't let this remark go. He quipped, "It may not be where they say it is, but I can tell you for sure that he's not buried in Williamsburg."

Rabbi Wein Stories Told on Himself

"When I was a young man in Chicago every *Succos* I tried to build my own *succah*. I always erected the *Succah* in time for the holiday, but at a great cost to my self-image and delicate fingers. Once I decided to hire a carpenter to help me. When the carpenter arrived he looked at my sorry set of tools and at the lumber I had collected. He assessed my competence with a withering remark: "Yungerman, shtell zich offen zeit, dus iz nisht a blatt gemorah; dus darf men kennen." ("Young man, stand aside, this is not a page of the Talmud; this is something you have to know how to do.")

❀ ❀ ❀

"Once I was engaged to deliver the main speech at a yeshiva in Brooklyn. This yeshiva was a very traditional Torah institution. Two of the alumni picked me up and on the way into the city I began to plan my speech.

"The foremost consideration of any speaker is to address the needs of his audience. I knew the history and traditions of this school and was planning a strategy that would appeal to that particular crowd. Just as we were settling into the monotony of the Palisades Parkway, I heard one of the alumni turn to the other and announce, 'Boruch Hashem, every year we get a different Rabbi for our dinner and what does he speak about? Torah, Torah, Torah. At least this year we'll give them a change of pace. Isn't that right, Rabbi Wein?'"

❀ ❀ ❀

"Every professional public speaker prides himself on his ability to sense when his speech has reached a climactic point. He knows how to marshal his rhetoric for a powerful conclusion. I remember vividly a synagogue dinner in Brooklyn when I had reached such a point in my speech. I took a long pause, which was to signal to everyone that I was about to say something very profound. Suddenly, a woman at one of the back tables got up from her seat and addressed a waiter who was making his way into the kitchen directly behind me. In a voice of tremendous clarity and volume she said, 'Waiter, you forgot the pickles again. Don't come back here without the pickles.'

"At that moment I understood what Moses must have felt like when the Jews complained about their cucumbers and watermelons."

※ ※ ※

"Sometimes rabbis get discouraged too. I remember once when things were pretty confusing. We had just relocated into our home in Monsey and cartons of books and kitchen dishes were strewn all over our living room. I was just about to start a new job. Transitions are always hard to make and they don't get any easier as one gets older.

"While we were still unpacking, a request from the County Department of Roads came in the mail. The County had decided to close off our block to through traffic and make our street a cul de sac. Now, the time had arrived to announce this news to the world. Since I happened to live in the first house on the block, the officials of the Highway Department came to me.

" 'We have to put up a sign, Rabbi,' the official began, 'to inform the driving public that your street is no longer a through street. Since your home is the first a driver will pass, the sign will be erected on your property.' I knew from experience as a lawyer that it wasn't going to do me any good to argue with this government official. The county has the right of *eminent domain* which entitles them to claim the first seven feet of one's lawn.

"He continued, 'We've got two kinds of signs for you to choose from. The first reads, *'No Outlet,'* the second says *'Dead End.'* Which would you prefer?'

"I considered the options. I had just abandoned a position in Florida. My new synagogue was located in the lower part of a house in Monsey, affectionately called 'Bais Ment,' and I hadn't yet unpacked. I was going through midcareer anxiety. The choice was clear.

" 'Sir,' I told the road man, 'I'll take the *'Dead End'* sign — it's more rabbinical!' " Now, visitors to my house probably don't notice the sign and the few who do don't appreciate the irony. I rarely inform them."

The Handkerchief

In Jewish law one way to transfer property is symbolically through a process called *kinyan sudar*. To perform this transfer or *kinyan* the buyer gives the seller an object, commonly a handkerchief, to act as the symbol of transfer. As the seller takes the handkerchief, ownership of the property being sold transfers to the buyer. The buyer at the same time, incurs the obligation of paying for the property. At this point the deal is *halachically* consummated and neither of the two parties, buyer nor seller, is allowed to renege.

A common usage of *kinyan sudar* is at a wedding. At the groom's table the Rabbi sits between the groom and the father of the bride. Here he presides, filling out the *kesubah* and the *tennaim* (contractual marriage documents) and having them properly signed. When the paperwork is finished the Rabbi passes a handkerchief to the groom who picks it up. He hands it back to the Rabbi who gives it to the bride's father to do the same. What is taking place is not some strange flag-waving ritual but a formal *kinyan* which seals the financial arrangements between the couple.

Another time when a *kinyan sudar* is necessary, is at the conclusion of civil court cases. Because of this Rabbi Wein offers his rabbinical students this sage advice: "As a Rabbi one should always carry a handkerchief in case he has to make a *kinyan sudar*. Of course he should always carry a handkerchief in case he has to polish his eyeglasses, or blow his nose, or whatever." After a brief pause he adds, "And preferably it should not be the same handkerchief."

Clarity

In Rockland County, there is a State psychiatric hospital that serves the emotionally unbalanced. A lady called up Rabbi Wein and introduced herself as an inmate .

"Are you the Rabbi Wein?" she asked.

"Yes," he answered.

"I live in Rockland State Hospital, and last night I had a vision and an angel instructed me to become Jewish."

"Did he give you my number also?" Rabbi Wein is always interested in helping the metaphysically inclined.

"Rabbi, I heard about you and I want to become Jewish. I'm serious."

"Well, I appreciate your interest but why don't you wait till you get out of the hospital and then maybe I can help you?" the Rabbi answered.

The woman didn't even pause to frame her answer, "But, Rabbi, only in here can I think clearly."

Sophistication

A woman was finally persuaded to attend a *Shabbos* synagogue service. That week the Torah reading recounted the beginning of the saga of Joseph and his brothers. As the woman listened to the Rabbi recount the dramatic story of how the brothers cast Joseph in the pit she began to cry. "How can brothers treat him like that?" she muttered to herself. When she heard how they sold him into slavery, she was moved and wept uncontrollably.

On the way home from synagogue her companion asked the woman what she felt about the services.

"I loved the services and especially the story about the brothers. It's just like real life. It could break your heart to see what brothers can do to each other," she replied, brushing away her tears.

The next year the same woman went to synagogue again and it happened they were reading the same portion. This time, however, listening to the same story she didn't cry at all. She sat there in stony silence throughout the reading.

When her friend asked her why she wasn't as emotionally involved as she was last year, she replied, "If that boy Joseph is going to start up with his brothers again, after what happened to him last year, why should I cry for him? By now he should know better."

Rabbi Wein used this story to make the point, "For Jews the Bible should be more than a story book."

The Rabbinate...
Or What's Left of It

On the day that President Kennedy got shot, a woman ran down the streets of Boro Park shouting, "The President's been shot, the President's been shot." Another woman thrust her head out an apartment window and cried hysterically, "Of which synagogue? Of which synagogue?"

❦ ❦ ❦

In Chicago there was a Conservative Rabbi who was a *Kohen* and therefore not allowed to preside at funerals. He felt he was suffering monetarily, so he took out an ad in the local Jewish papers announcing that he was resigning from the *Kehunah* (the priestly class).

"I wonder who is going to accept his letter of resignation," Rabbi Wein questions, "Aaron HaKohen?"

❦ ❦ ❦

Twenty-seven percent of Reform rabbis profess atheism to be their religious belief!?

❦ ❦ ❦

Two religious leaders were discussing spiritual affairs, and one was heard to remark: " . . . But what if there is a God?"

❦ ❦ ❦

At the leading Reform seminary, The Hebrew Union College, 70% of all entering rabbinical students are women. Rabbi Wein spoke recently in N.Y.U. close to where the Jewish Institute of Religion, the other Reform seminary is located. He observed that women outnumber the men studying to become cantors or rabbis.

"Most of those wearing yarmulkas on that campus were women. At the Conservative college, the Jewish Theological Seminary, nearly two-thirds of all candidates for the clergy are female. *Halachic* problems are not the only problems afflicting the march of women to the pulpit. The sociological impact has yet to be registered or understood."

☙ ☙ ☙

Until the Fourteenth Century rabbis did not receive any pay for their labors. They supported themselves as business people or as artisans. In most American Orthodox synagogues nowadays, there is a movement afoot to return to that pay scale.

The Rabbi Goes on Strike

Rabbi Eliyahu Dovid Rabinowitz-Tumim was known simply by his acronym, the *Aderes*. At one time he held the position of Rav in Mir and Ponevezhe a sizable city in Poland. For some reason the congregants in the community forgot to pay their Rav his salary for sixteen weeks.

The *Aderes* appealed to his congregation to pay him his due, and when they put him off, he did what workers have done since time immemorial — he withheld his services. In other words, he went on strike. He decided no *halachic* questions, he canceled all his lectures and refused to minister to the needs of the community.

Eventually, the townspeople realized that they could only hold out for so long and they paid him his back salary and kept him current from then on.

The $150,000 Rabbi

On a trip last year to a large North American city to raise money for his yeshiva, Rabbi Wein was queried by the President of a local synagogue he was addressing if he knew of an experienced middle-aged Rabbi for a full-time position with a large and affluent congregation. Always the consummate professional, Rabbi Wein was curious about the wages and benefits. The synagogue member estimated that for a man comparable to Rabbi Wein, $125,000 would be fair compensation. Rabbi Wein thought about it and made some suggestions.

The man was not impressed with Rabbi Wein's candidates. "Would **you** be interested in the position, Rabbi Wein? Because if you take the job, maybe we could get you $150,000." Rabbi was silent. The President added, "Is that too little?"

Rabbi Wein thought about the offer and replied. "No, it's definitely not too little, but I have a feeling it may be too much."

When the Bais Torah members heard the punchline, they laughed, albeit a little nervously. Rabbi Wein was quick to reassure them. "Don't worry, you guys have nothing to be concerned about. I'm not going anywhere."

9

The Mussar Shmooze

A lot of people worry about their frumkeit (religious level) and that of others. Rabbi Wein's teacher used to say, "Jews shouldn't get nervous about being frum — frum is a galoch. (Religiosity, piety, is a Catholic Priest.)

This pithy remark went to the heart of the matter. Judaism is very complex and Jews need to be more sophisticated in their appraisal of piety.

The Mussar Shmooze

ussar — literally, chastisement — took on new meaning in the nineteenth century with the birth of the *Mussar* Movement which aimed to deepen the religious commitment and values of the Jewish community. To quote Rabbi Wein's book, *Triumph of Survival* (pg. 192):

"Mussar was not mere piety. It was psychology, sociology, and philosophy as well . . . [It] taught that salvation lay in a Torah society founded on moral standards set by the Torah and Jewish tradition. Much like Chassidus, the language and outer garb of *mussar* were new, but its internal core was as old as Sinai . . . [It] required punctilious observance of the law and its commandments, but with a soul; with the understanding that good deeds are necessary to create a good person, and that becoming a good person was the end goal of Jewish life."

Although Rabbi Yisroel Salanter, founder of the *Mussar* Movement, expected the masses to adopt the movement, in reality, it was a movement that appealed primarily to scholarly, intellectual people. One of the main areas of concentration of *mussar* was in the Lithuanian yeshivas of the nineteenth and twentieth centuries. Today, the *mussar shmooze* (talk) is a standard feature of the contemporary yeshiva. The *shmooze* can be fiery and ignite the emotions, or reflective and stimulate serious thought, but whatever the form, the end goal is the same: to make us pause for a moment in order to help us break the shackles of habit and affect a change for the better.

The Main Task in Life

The following talk is excerpted from one of Rabbi Wein's weekly mussar shmoozes to his students at Shaarei Torah.

"The main task in life is simple, deceptively simple. It is to 'stay alone.' If you can stay alone you will not cause pain to another human being. This is the *pshat* (plain meaning) in what

Hillel told the convert who asked to be taught the whole Torah on one foot (i.e. summarized its main message as briefly as possible), "treat others as you would have them treat you." And that's it. That is life's main rule. Stay by yourself and don't cause pain to another human being. Take note because these ideas are basically interconnected.

"But as with all simple maxims, it's very hard to translate this into practical behavior, especially when your neighbor wants what you want.

"Someone called the other night and wanted me to conduct a *din Torah* (adjudication in a Jewish court). What was the problem? It seems he and another fellow both wanted to buy the same house. I found out a little more about the house and where it was located. I knew there was a better lot on the same block, and I knew what this fellow was going to do with this house once he bought it. It cost $350,000 and he was going to buy it and tear it down. That's the latest Monsey style. You have to buy a house for $350,000 and then tear it down. Then you build another house because who could live in that old house that you just paid so much money for?

"So, why don't you buy the house next door or the lot down the block," I recommended innocently. (The first rule in conducting a *din Torah* is to try to defuse the situation so that there is no need for the *din Torah*) But all my advice went for naught. He said he wanted this particular house and his wife wouldn't be happy unless he would get this house. But he didn't want the house. What he really wanted is that the other fellow not get it. That's really what was driving him up the wall! He just didn't want this other fellow to have it.

"And if you think about it, outrageous as it may seem, a lot of our lives are spent trying to make sure that others don't achieve their goals. A lot of our time is thrown away making reckonings on the affairs of others. A person achieves greatness when he completely isolates himself from others. Once isolated, he won't envy others and if he's not envious, he probably won't cause others any harm either. That's the way to stay out of trouble. Stay away from it. Don't become a recluse, but stay by yourself. It sounds paradoxical but I'll provide some examples.

"My Rebbe, Rabbi Chaim Kreisworth, tells a *moshol* (parable) about this. Two people had the same kind of store in the same neighborhood. One store was extremely successful and one barely survived. After a couple of years, the unsuccessful storeowner came into his rival's store and asked him pointedly, 'I know it's none of my business, but we have the same goods, sell for practically the same price, and we're open about the same amount of time. How come you're so successful and I'm not?'

"The other person answered him, 'You know what the difference is? I'm successful because I'm just watching one store and you're watching two stores. You're so worried about my store that you don't have time to develop your own store. You're too busy competing with me to pay proper attention to what you have to do.'

"That's the key. Be scrupulously careful to tend to your business. Watching what others are doing causes you to judge them, to compete with them, and to envy them. When you're not content with what you have, then you have put yourself in a position to harm others. Staying out of trouble gets fairly complex at times. Nobody wants to be a hermit, cut off from society. Yet if you continuously immerse yourself in the waters of society one day you'll find you can't get back to shore."

❦ ❦ ❦

"There's no way to give *mussar* to others until you live this *mussar* yourself. Most of the time we walk around as if we were innocent of any crime. We aren't aware of the harm we cause. One must look in the mirror and see the harm we cause others, then we can teach others not to cause harm. If you want to say *mussar* over to others, say *mussar* to yourself.

"However, I warn you, it's not as simple as it sounds. Most people who think they have the right to chastise others are probably people who don't have that right. And conversely, the only people who have this right are those who think they don't have the right.

"It's one of the paradoxical situations in life. I am reminded of Groucho Marx's great bad joke. He sent a letter of resignation to an organization saying 'I refuse to belong to any club that would accept me as member.' People who feel far from perfect are on the road to perfection and those who feel themselves to be accomplished *mussar* masters need to check themselves for a spiritual overhaul.

"One's goal should be not to harm others. If a person can achieve that, then he'll be saved from lots of problems in this world and the next."

The Butcher's Complaint

There's a famous story told about Rabbi Chaim Soloveitchik which illustrates the problem of keeping ones emotional distance. In Brisk, Reb Chaim was the Rav and presided as the spiritual leader of the community. When it came to adjudicating *halachic* questions, however, the people used a very special man to decide their questions, Rav Simcha Zelig. Rav Simcha Zelig decided all matters of kashruth, issues of family purity, and money disputes.

Reb Simcha Zelig was noted to be an astute judge and his reputation for fairness carried well beyond the borders of Brisk. Reb Chaim was grateful to have such a respected scholar in residence. The two of them worked very well together, and even shared the same office in the synagogue building.

Once it happened in Brisk, before the holiday of Shavuos, that one of the local butchers bought at a great expense a very large bull which he slaughtered for the retail trade. When they opened the bull up to examine its carcass they found lesions on the lungs. This finding brought the Kosher status of the animal into question. Therefore they brought the animal before Rav Simcha Zelig.

He worked on the question all night trying to find a way to mitigate the problems, but they were too formidable. In the morning he came to Reb Chaim and said that he looked through everything, but couldn't do anything with it. "It's not kosher," he said.

Reb Chaim accepted his findings and called in the butcher to tell him the sad news. The butcher listened without blinking and responded, "If that's what you found, then it's acceptable to me." He would now have to sell the animal to the gentile trade at a loss, yet he accepted his fate graciously.

Later that summer the same butcher had a dispute with another Jew concerning an old debt. It was of small monetary consequence, a matter of less than a hundred dollars. They agreed to come before Rav Simcha Zelig to adjudicate the dispute. In Reb Chaim Brisker's office, both sides presented their cases and he rendered his judgment. "You, butcher, have to pay this man the money in full."

The butcher was furious. He got up from the table and cursed Rav Simcha Zelig, the adjudicator. Reb Chaim, who was present and a very gentle person by nature, was shocked. He stood up and slapped the butcher, then he threw him out. "*Gay arois fun bais din, gay arois fun bais din shteibel. Mechutzef, mechutzef.*" (Get out of here! Get out of this court! You disrespectful person!)

Months passed and Yom Kippur arrived. After the final meal before the fast, Reb Chaim and his sons were readying themselves to go to synagogue when Reb Chaim recalled the unpleasant incident. He said to his sons, "Remember this summer we had an unpleasant matter with the butcher. He cursed Rav Zelig and I threw him out. Maybe I shouldn't have been so harsh with him? I think now I shouldn't have done it. Where does he pray? I'm going to beg forgiveness from him."

Reb Chaim inquired after his whereabouts and set out to find him. It was already time for *Kol Nidre* and his own congregation was waiting for him to begin services. Nevertheless, he looked around until he found the butcher in the back of a small synagogue.

"Do you remember," he asked, "in the summer you had a case with Rav Simcha Zelig. The Rav decided against you and it so displeased you that you cursed him. Then I slapped you and called you an impudent person and threw you out?"

The butcher barely nodded. "Well, I shouldn't have done it, so I am asking you to forgive me."

"No, Rebbe," the butcher shot back. "I won't forgive you."

Again Reb Chaim calmly made his request, "Do you remember this summer you had a court case with Rav Simcha Zelig and he decided against you and it disturbed you so much that you cursed him. I slapped you and called you impudent and I threw you out of the court. I shouldn't have done it, and I beg you to forgive me."

The butcher shook his head. "No," and he looked away from the Rabbi.

A third time, Reb Chaim made his appeal, and this time the butcher looked him straight in the eye and said to him, "Rabbi, you can ask me forever, but I'm not going to give you forgiveness."

Reb Chaim said, "Three times I asked you to forgive me and you refused me each time. According to *halachah*, I'm not required to do more than that, so the problem is yours now." With that he left.

All of Brisk heard the story and the night Yom Kippur was over Rav Simcha Zelig came into the room where Reb Chaim was sitting. "I am baffled. Before Shavuos, the butcher came to us with the case of an unkosher bull, which cost him greatly, and he accepted the loss calmly. Later this summer I decided against him again for far less money and he cursed me and then refused to grant you forgiveness on Yom Kippur. To such an extent is his bitterness — it doesn't make sense?"

Reb Chaim shook his head sadly, "I'm afraid that's human nature," he began. "When you decided that the bull was unkosher he could accept it and that was that. In his mind he was a righteous person. What could he do? He was out some money and he'd have to make it up. But he knew his children wouldn't starve and there'll be plenty of work for him to do tomorrow.

"In the second case," Reb Chaim explained, "it wasn't the money that bothered him. It was the fact that his adversary won! He couldn't stand that his enemy won. That he wouldn't forgive. That he can't overcome. And that's our nature; that's how we deal with people — that's why we have problems."

Leitzonis

Although he is endowed with a ready wit and a dry, sophisticated sense of humor, Rabbi Wein is quick to point out that "kidding around" can cause a great deal of pain. There is a world of difference between harmless kidding and thoughtless sarcasm. "With the power of *leitzonis* (mockery) everything can come crashing down." Thus warns the *Mesillas Yeshorim* (a great mussar work).

Leitzonis is not simply a matter of cracking jokes; it is best understood as scoffing, the kind of corrosive, destructive humor so popular in our culture. "We certify this type of invidious sarcasm when we use or listen to 'ethnic humor,'" Rabbi Wein warns. "When the ethnics are us, suddenly, it's no longer funny; it's something else." ("How did you feel when you heard the riddle, 'What's the thinnest book in the library?' and the answer was 'The Jewish Book of Ethics!'")

In the first verse of Psalms, King David puts scoffers in the ranks of the wicked and sinful: "Praiseworthy is the man who walked not in the counsel of the wicked, and stood not in the path of the sinful, and sat not in the session of the scornful." Rabbi Wein relates that while he was Rabbi in Miami Beach, he had a congregant who always came late to the Sabbath services.

"He would saunter in toward the end of the Torah reading (past the middle of the service), week after week. One year, Passover Eve fell on a *Shabbos* and in order to finish destroying the *chometz* (leavened bread) on time, morning services began very early, around six in the morning. At 7:15, in he walked, right in the middle of reading the Torah. At that point it became obvious that it wasn't just a matter of tardiness or sleeping late; he came late on purpose. He just didn't like sitting through the whole service, praying for that length of time."

So Rabbi Wein went to work. He spoke to the man and pointed out the benefits of full concentration on one's prayers. He explained that the service was built very carefully. He reasoned that one cannot be a part-time supplicant, the Almighty wants serious effort. Rabbi Wein cajoled and argued until one morning his efforts carried the day and he persuaded his member to work on coming to synagogue on time. Sure enough that Shabbos morning he showed up late but earlier than usual.

But no sooner did he arrive at his seat than the *leitzonim* (scoffers) went to work.

"What's the matter? Couldn't sleep."

"Hey, did your wife throw you out of the house?"

"Hey, is your clock broken; it's only nine."

That's all it took. "He never came on time again," Rabbi Wein says, "and I never spoke to him about it any more. But this time it's on the other guys' *cheshbon* (heavenly account). They bought it, not me."

It's No Trick

It is reported that every so often, the Vilna Gaon sought constructive criticism. He felt the need to sharpen his understanding of himself and wanted an objective appraisal of his faults.

The only trouble was — who was going to play the role of critic to this towering personage? Who had the necessary expertise and confidence to risk pointing out the shortcomings of such a great man? The Vilna Gaon was the spiritual leader of all Ashkenazic Jewry and his command of the Torah was so great who would have the *chutzpah* to critique such a giant?

The only man in Europe the Gaon trusted to be ruthlessly honest with him was the Maggid of Dubno (Rabbi Yaakov Krantz), the world famous *tzaddik* who used to deliver *mussar* sermons traveling throughout Europe. Only the Maggid, a great man in his own right, was sufficiently knowledgeable and courageous to tell the Gaon the truth about himself. Despite the honor, he didn't relish the encounter. He knew the Gaon was a giant of a personality who didn't suffer fools lightly. So he chose those stories which attacked the Gaon where he was strongest yet most vulnerable, the ivory tower of his intellectual grandeur.

"You must think very highly of yourself sitting here in your study, protected from the world. What a fine image you must have of yourself, so refined and holy. We all wish we could be as spiritually self-sufficient as you seem to be."

The Gaon listened willingly, as the Maggid continued. "You know, of course, you stand head and shoulders above everyone; nobody in the world would dare challenge you." Now the Maggid began to warm to his task. "Every day of your life, people must tell you how marvelous are. What an agreeable way to live, learning all day and letting a few people in at night for questions. It must make you feel exalted."

The *mussar* master knew his trade and his gently sarcastic tone was making inroads. "What an outrageous way to live; you're so important you can even have a *mussar* lesson brought right into your study by none other than the Maggid of Dubno. You don't have to stand in line for anything."

The Maggid concluded: "Go outside, my friend, and see what it's like out there. See if you can sustain your level of learning while you're sweeping out a store or trying to sew a button on a coat, or dealing with an irate customer. The marketplace is a noisy, rough-and-tumble place. Here, in the sanctity of your room, it's no trick to live like a prince. Come outside for a month and try to live by your wits. That would be a real *kuntz* — a trick."

The Maggid's words had hit home — the Gaon was weeping copiously. The Maggid left the room to get the great man some water and when he returned the Vilna Gaon tearfully thanked him. The *mussar* session was concluded. After a bit, when he had composed himself, the Gaon walked with the Maggid down the stairs and out into the street. On the bustling street corner he looked down the avenue which faced the central marketplace.

The Vilna Gaon said, "You're right. It is very noisy here and it must be terribly hard to make a living. But," he motioned to his window on the second floor, "I want you to understand something. What I do up there in my room, *mein lernen, iz oich a kuntz.*" ("My learning is also a trick.") He shook the Maggid's hand and repeated with a sigh, "Thank you," and he repeated, *"es iz oich a kuntz"* ("It's also some trick.") An alternate tradition is that the Gaon said, "You are right, it is no trick to remain in my room. But who says that one has to perform tricks?"

From the way he uttered those words, the Maggid understood how much the Gaon must have suffered to acquire his vast learning.

The Oldest Jew

"In Miami," Rabbi Wein said, "I met a lot of elderly people. The oldest Jew I knew belonged to my synagogue. He had become wealthy by investing in New Jersey real estate. His specialty was parking lots and he acquired many of them. He was 96 when he told me his story, and was enjoying his retirement in

Florida to the fullest. He didn't pass on until eight years later, after I left Miami to come to Monsey.

"Once," Rabbi Wein reported, "I found myself sitting next to him at a wedding reception and asked him the reasons for his long life. He launched into his tale with gusto."

" 'I was born in Russia in 1875,' he reported, 'and lived there until a pogrom forced me to leave just after my bar mitzvah. I don't know the reason for the pogrom, but they didn't need any reason to murder Jews. They killed both my parents and I fled heartbroken and penniless to Lithuania. I was in desperate straits. Those were turbulent times and I didn't know a soul. Who had time for an orphan? So I came to Kovno which I knew to be a Jewish city, a stronghold of Torah and charity.

" 'I was adopted by students of a *mussar* school run by Rabbi Itzele Peterburger. I remember this man vividly — he was the strongest man I ever met and yet the most gentle. He made a wonderful bar-mitzvah for me. He even taught me how to tie my *tefillin* and read the Torah. He was such a kind man that I longed to be around him. Sometimes, though, I expressed my feeling too strongly.

I needed a little warmth, so I would reach out to touch him and in my haste would rip his clothing by mistake. Or I would see him across a room, run over to him and give him a bump instead of an embrace. I just couldn't stop myself from grabbing at him as he walked past me — I was simply a very klutzy teenager.

" 'In my second year in his yeshiva, Rav Itzele was the *chazan* on Yom Kippur. He sang wonderfully. Most of the time he would chant melodies he made up himself. They were so sweet, one would have needed a steel heart to keep from crying. When the service was over, he led the yeshiva in a festive dance.

" 'I guess the long fast and the joy of watching my Rabbi dance around with the boys made me so happy I was almost dizzy with joy. I only knew I wanted desperately to hold on to him. Pushing the boys aside, I rushed through the crowd and started to dance with my beloved Rabbi. While we were whirling around, in my frenzy, I must have accidentally kicked him very hard because he stopped dancing and hopped around on one foot while he rubbed his shin. He cupped my face lovingly in his hands and said, *'Kind, lang zolst du leben ober brikell nisht mit daine fiis.'* ('Child, long shall you live, but please never kick with your feet.') So that was it. Reb Itzele blessed me eighty years ago, and that's why I'm still here.'

"With that," Rabbi Wein related, "the old man lifted his glass of wine and shouted *L'chaim!*" Rabbi Wein smiled, got up, and approached the dance floor to partake in the joyousness of the wedding.

❦ ❦ ❦

"Whenever I see a Jew who is preserved into a robust old age," Rabbi Wein said, "I reflect on the value of Jewish blessings."

"I am reminded of Yaakov *Avinu* (Jacob, our father). To escape the famine, Joseph brings him down to Egypt. When he is introduced to Pharaoh, Yaakov is asked to give Egypt his blessing. Yaakov obliges, and we are told the Nile River overflowed its banks and the cycle of fertility and abundance returned to Egypt. The blessing of our father nullified the worldwide famine.

"Hasn't this been our story too? For 3,300 years the Jewish people have blessed the world with their genius and the world has reaped gigantic benefits. Where we have been invited in and welcomed, our presence brought national success. When we were rejected and expelled, we left failure and ruin in our wake. Consider the fate of all the empires which have spurned us. Who has survived *our* expulsion?

"From the scraps of the Jewish table, we have fed the world with our spirit, ideas, and inventiveness. The world denies us at its peril. Even the left-handed compliment of a *tzaddik* in a bygone age can produce enough blessing to carry an awkward orphan ahead to a new land and an eventful, prosperous life."

Tikkun

Everyone can do *teshuvah* (increase their sincere observance). The moment you say that you can't, you can't. The same with learning and personality, "I can't learn this," or "I can't be a good person." Even when there's no way out, there's a way out. If you want to repair yourself the Almighty will let you.

There's a Chassidic statement, "It came to its *tikkun*." This means it came to its corrected road. There's nothing that is hopeless or lost. In kabbalah, evil is defined as imperfect good. Even with a convert who dies without heirs and there's no way to make financial reparation for a sin committed against him — let's say a theft — the thief can make restitution by bringing a guilt offering to the Temple. Therefore, there are no hopeless situations.

Vintage Wein

Don't confuse Jews and Judaism. Just because you see a Jew do something wrong, don't blame God; don't blame Torah.

※ ※ ※

Reform Judaism came to reform Judaism. Mussar came to reform Jews.

※ ※ ※

Technology changes, civilization changes, society changes, but the basic nature of people rarely changes.

❦ ❦ ❦

The great balancing act in life is to know who you are and not get depressed by that knowledge.

❦ ❦ ❦

We all have private demons; that's part of life. How we deal with them determines who we are.

❦ ❦ ❦

If I haven't been able to have a feeling of self-worth in this world, I won't have it in the next world.

❦ ❦ ❦

No two people are alike. When a person is important he does things importantly; when he feels unimportant he does things unimportantly. Everybody's name is in G-d's book, but we each write our own chapter in that book.

Three-Ring Circus

"Life is like a three-ring circus. There are many things happening at once, and a person has to know what to look at. Some of my grandchildren went to see the circus. The older ones enjoyed it, but the four-year-old came home crying. He was so confused by all that was going on he couldn't have a good time. Every time he concentrated on one thing he missed another and naturally did not see some of the most exciting parts of the circus. His attention was always focused elsewhere.

"Our society is very similar. People are always missing the main event. We don't know what to watch. So we watch the Knicks. But the Knicks are not what life is all about.

"While the Israeli government whisked off the Ethiopian Jews to *Eretz Yisroel*, the rest of the world was watching the Ethiopian rebels take over the country. They did not realize that God directed that whole scenario just to get the Jews out. After 15,000 Jews left Ethiopia, the dictator was deposed. He served his purpose, so he's gone. Everything is because of Israel (*Hakol beshvil Yisrael*).

"The Soviet Union lies in ruins. Why, if not so that millions of Jews could escape to the Holy Land? But all the media wants to talk about is Gorbachev and Yeltsin. Gorbachev himself didn't know he is just a pawn in God's master plan.

"*Hakol beshvil Yisrael.* Whatever happens in the world is for Jews. They don't teach that in the New York Times, but it's absolutely true. Our problem is that most of the time we look at the wrong thing; we are completely enthralled by the minor attraction on the card."

Fish Paper

When Ivan Boesky (a wealthy secular Jew) was being tried for stock fraud, he had the good fortune that Reagan was implicated in the sale of arms to Iran. His story is over now; they're wrapping fish in it already. The world is fickle.

Sportorama

Sportorama is a Monsey sports and health facility, which specializes in cardiac care.

For health reasons, Rabbi Wein attends an exercise class during the week. This particular class is mostly gentile so when the Rabbi first displayed his *tzitzis* as he exercises, they provoke interest and his colleagues on the treadmills start asking him questions.

"What's that?" one asks, pointing at his *tzitzis*.

Rather than answer the question directly, Rabbi Wein points to the man's special belt which measured his heart rate and hooked him up through various wires to a computer which monitored vital functions throughout his body. "What are you wearing that for?" he asks back.

"Come on, Rabbi, don't play games. You know that's the monitor: you wear one, too. How can you exercise without the monitor?"

Rabbi Wein held up his *tzitzis* and explained, "Well, this is our monitor. We wear a monitor all the time; we can't live our life without being monitored."

"Yeah, but what are you hooked up to?"

"I'm glad you asked," Rabbi Wein said puffing. "It's hooked up to the ultimate monitor." The Rabbi pointed up to the ceiling of Sportorama: "And it's always measuring how well we are doing."

They chuckled in disbelief.

"It's true," Rabbi Wein continued. "Just look around you. In our class, we all have our strings and our wires hooked into our exercise belt which receives these wires and relays them to a master computer full of other strings and wires — blue ones and red ones. No one can explain how it works. There are lawyers and doctors here; very smart people in the class and nobody asks to explain their wires. Nobody says a word. The instructions say to put on the monitor and you do it even if you do not understand how it works. But my little strings produce disbelief.

"At least I know why I wear my *tzitzis*. A person may find himself about to do something he shouldn't and the *tzitzis* will itch and remind him — and hopefully stop him. A person has to know he is always being monitored."

❦ ❦ ❦

Rabbi Wein used the Sportorama story to make a point to his yeshiva students:

Rabbi Yisroel Salanter describes a person's mind as a raging river flooding its banks. As long as we're alive, it's always flowing. Even at night it doesn't let us rest. How are we able to control the flood of dangerous thoughts that threaten to destroy us? It is written that the *mitzvos* of *tzitzis* and *tefillin* are antidotes for this problem.

According to the *Zohar*, *tzitzis* is the whip that reminds us who we are. Our minds are flooded with provocative thoughts and we are saturated with fantasy twenty-four hours a day. Yet this simple garment is worn as a reminder to restrain the drives that threaten to tear us apart.

What are *tzitzis* for? Perhaps Hitler said it best:

"In nature there is no pity for the lesser creatures when they are destroyed, so that the fittest may survive. Going against nature brings ruin to man . . . It is only Jewish impudence to demand that we overcome Nature!"

The Acquisitive Desire

Thank God, we have been blessed with an abundance of wealth in America. A family can eat out at a different restaurant each night, Chinese, Mexican, Italian, etc. But that's the problem: the more there are, the less satisfied we are. Before Passover, Rabbi Wein was at the liquor store to buy some mead for *Yom Tov* when a lady walked in to buy wine. She spent some time just walking around the store and marveling at all the varieties and different brands of wine. There must have been over 140 different types. She could not decide what she wanted, what her husband wanted, what her guests might want, what wines were proper for the Seder and which for the rest of the meals. Finally, in exasperation, she said, "It was better when there was only one wine."

Rabbi Wein observes, "She's right, even though that one wine was a sweet, heavy Malaga that knocked you out after the first cup. The abundance and variety itself leaves one unfulfilled — it's too much. The moment there are so many, then the one you have is not good enough."

"When Henry Ford came out with the Model-T, the first car available to the average consumer at a cost of $350, he said "They can have it in whatever color they want as long as it's black." That's unimaginable today. It is impossible to buy a car today without feeling you were cheated and maybe missed a better one. As soon as you drive out of the lot, you are unhappy.

"I was looking for a word processor recently, and I went to the store to get an idea of what I was getting into. Naturally, I didn't have a clue as to what I needed but after a while, looking at the descriptions of the models, I began to get a feel for it. I walked over to the salesperson and pointed out a certain model. He smiled at me and said, 'Whatever you get, you'll have to come back anyway. By next year newer ones will have arrived and everything you see in this room will be obsolete.'

"What can you do after a comment like that? If you buy it,

you feel like an idiot; if you don't, it's another year of writing by hand.

"In life, it is crucial not to be swallowed up by the sheer volume of everything available. No person will ever get all the things in life that he wants because as the possessions increase the desire for more, better things increases. There was a popular bumper sticker not too many years ago: "WHOEVER DIES WITH THE MOST TOYS WINS." That sums up our society.

"Therefore, a person must work very hard to keep perspective on what is truly meaningful in life. One must strive to build for permanence and everlasting importance. If you are traveling to *Eretz Yisrael*, don't complain about the airline food. If God is taking you by the hand to a place of destiny, don't wail about the imperfect conditions. Only through conquering the acquisitive desire can a person see those goals clearly."

Simplicity

When Rabbi Wein first moved to Monsey, he prayed at Community Synagogue, Rabbi Moshe Tendler's synagogue. One evening, Rabbi Tendler was out of town, but his world renowned father-in-law, Rabbi Moshe Feinstein *zt'l*, was at the *minyan*.

"There were about twelve people there," Rabbi Wein recalls. "Most of them came in off the street just to say *kaddish*. Between *minchah* and *maariv* there was a short break and Rav Moshe would not allow it to be frittered away. So he pulled a *Chumash* (Five Books of Moses) down from the shelf and began teaching from it to the small crowd in the room. He read each verse and then translated it into Yiddish with such a simple quality. He didn't say any great Torah thoughts; no deep analyses from the commentators; just the plain words. "*Vayomer* — *un ehr hot gezokt*' (And he said). But he spoke in such a way that he wasn't talking down to anyone. Great people have that ability to talk to everyone: children, teenagers, adults. There are people who won't give a class if there are less than 9,000 people — all scholars — in attendance. Insecure people can only teach on the highest levels, but a truly great person is able to teach *alef-bais* (elementary subjects like the alphabet) also.

※ ※ ※

"A Rav in Europe once wrote to Rav Kook asking his advice about moving to *Eretz Yisrael*. In a famous letter, Rav Kook answered him, 'If you are prepared to come and be a grocery man, then by all means move. But if you want the honor you currently receive in Lithuania, then don't even think about it.'"

"Rav Kook was not criticizing the Rav; he was just explaining the reality. Similarly, in these times, what prevents American Jews from settling in Israel and making *aliyah?* Not enough money, or not enough honor? The Chofetz Chaim, the greatest of men and most pious of Jews, was a simple person by nature. A small man who grew up in a small town, he never held an official position nor was he the student of a great teacher, nor did he study in a great yeshiva. And that is why he was such a holy man. The Chofetz Chaim befriended the lower classes — the peasants and unskilled laborers. He gave them classes in *halachah*, *Chumash*, and *mussar*. As they were uneducated, he did not teach them heavier subjects. He stayed at their level.

"Why was Moses the most humble of all men? Because he was the greatest of all men. Humility only becomes the great ones.

Naivete

One of the qualities found in great leaders is a certain measure of naivete. Moses asked the Children of Israel a rhetorical question: "What does God want of you, but to fear Him?" The Talmud asks: "Is fear of Heaven such a small request that Moses could treat it so simply?" The answer is that for Moses fear of heaven was so very natural that it was difficult for him to imagine living otherwise. The greatness of such people is that they do not know how great they are.

Rabbi Wein remembers one of those special mentors in the Chicago yeshiva he attended as a teenager. "He was the first person I ever saw who could learn four hours straight without moving from his seat. He would walk into the study hall in the afternoon, sit down, open his text and learn — for four hours straight. This Rabbi learned twenty-six hours out of twenty-four.

"One Fourth of July, the boys in the class planned a field trip after yeshiva was out. We wanted to go on an outing, probably a visit to Lake Michigan or to the Museum of Science and Industry or maybe to a Chicago Cubs doubleheader. As soon as class was over, our Rabbi saw that we were all hurrying to get out and he asked us where we were going that was so important. Now, how do you explain to your Rabbi about Wrigley Field? That was simply beyond him. So we just told him that we had to go somewhere, because for this Rabbi if you had the whole afternoon off, it was inconceivable that it would not be spent sitting and learning in the study hall. But we were fifteen years old, and that way of thinking was not yet a part of us — but he eventually influenced all of us, though none of us ever matched his devotion to study."

Forest Lawn

In Forest Lawn Cemetery, the Hollywood version of a cemetery, many famous movie stars are buried. One of the most famous is Al Jolson. On almost half an acre of land, he is interred in a magnificent mausoleum landscaped with a large pond containing real Japanese fish. It is maintained in luxury and throughout that section of the cemetery, his recorded songs play continuously over a loudspeaker.

In another plot not too far away, a man is buried in his Roll Royce. He has no coffin; they just strapped him behind the wheel and buried him with the car. He must feel that he is taking his *olam hazeh* (rewards of this life) with him and if he is privileged to reach *olam habah* (rewards of the coming world) at least he's ready to take a spin. Your soul is not proud of your automobile.

Shmeck Taback

Rabbi Kook, the Chief Rabbi of Rechovoth, Israel, told this story to Rabbi Wein on one of his trips to Israel.

"Every Jewish small town in Europe had one or two *"meshugaim."* We also have them here in the United States. They're called, 'homeless,' 'disadvantaged,' or 'unstable.' The difference between modern *meshugaim* and those old time *meshugaim* is that the old timers stood in synagogue a whole day and knew all the Psalms by heart and felt they were part of the social world. The town would manufacture small tasks for them to perform that made them feel wanted. They sat in synagogues all day and emptied a spitoon every couple of hours. They were nonviolent and nobody was afraid of them.

"American *meshugaim*, on the other hand, are a different breed. Look at them the wrong way and they take out a knife. Society's *meshugaim* reflect the values of that society. In the modern world, *meshugaim* kill because society kills. The *meshugaim* in Lithuania used to spend their time finding riddles based on *parshat hashevua* (weekly Bible chapter).

"How great are the differences between generations!"

※ ※ ※

"In Radun, one of these characters went by the name of Avraham Tzwantzig, Abraham Twenty, so called because he could only count up to the number 20. One summer day, he disappeared from the town. He didn't show up in synagogue and couldn't be found in the streets. He was missing two or three days when the Jews in town went around and asked the gentiles if they had seen him. "Maybe he fell into the river?" they answered.

After about ten days, he came back and everybody gathered around him, asking where he had been.

"I went on a trip," he replied.

"Where did you go, Avraham?"

"I went to Kovno." Kovno was the largest city in Lithuania. "I went to the fair."

"Everyone was excited by this news. In those days, big city fairs were wondrous spectacles. This *meshuganah* had done something truly adventurous.

"What did you do there?" they asked.

He took out of his pocket a little box of snuff and said, "I bought a *shmeck taback* (snuff of tabacco)."

They all laughed. "You went all the way to Kovno to buy a *shmeck taback*? You could buy a *shmeck taback* in Radun. You traveled to the big city to buy a bit of snuff?" (In our country, it would be similar to going to a World's Fair and bringing back an ice cream).

The children of the town flew through the neighborhoods to spread the word that Avraham Tzwantzig had come home. The story of his trip to the big city eventually reached the ears of the Chofetz Chaim. When he heard that the poor soul went to the big city and all he brought back was a *shmeck tabac*, the great Rabbi sat down at his kitchen table and wept bitterly.

His grandchildren were puzzled, "*Zayde*," they asked, "What are you crying about?"

"*Kinderlach*," he said, "the *Gemara* (Talmud) says that each one of the souls that comes to this world must travel 500 hundred million galaxies to get here. A soul travels so far to find a body and what does it wind up with? What is its reward? A *shmeck taback*. Such a long trip for a little box of snuff!"

The Chofetz Chaim was not only referring to the town fool, he was talking about people in general. We are all Avraham Tzwantzigs searching for our pitiful "good time."

※ ※ ※

Having a "good time" is a major industry in the United States. Billions of dollars are spent convincing people to "enjoy" themselves. But the soul that comes 500 hundred million galaxies is not impressed.

"I brought back for my three-year-old grandson in America a present from Israel and he played with it for ten minutes before putting it aside. He was through with it in no time and was bored again. We've got the VCR, compact disks, Disneyworld. What's next? For a soul to come all that way to get a box of snuff is something to cry over."

※ ※ ※

"The purpose of a yeshiva is to give the students more than a *shmeck taback*. I always tell the students, 'If it were up to me, I would delay the bar-mitzvah till a person is forty-three. If you take a boy of thirteen and tell him about the obligations of Torah, what does he make of it? He's more interested in the second round draft choice of the Miami Heat. Why are parents buying him a *Mishna Brurah*, a *Rambam*? Get him season's tickets!

"By the time you're forty-three, you've calmed down a little. A lot of things don't bother you any more. You learn Torah with a sense of purpose, a sense of accomplishment.

"Unfortunately, the reality is that the most important decisions are made at an age when people are least qualified to make them. The choice of whom you marry, for instance, is often made early and many times for the wrong reasons. Young people look for things that are not lasting and don't really go to the heart of the matter.

"When you choose a career thirty years from now you're going to be doing it. You're going to get up in the morning and wish that you didn't have to go to work that day. 'Dear God, why do I have to go to work today? I have no interest in it. Why did I ever become . . .? I'm tired of being an accountant, a lawyer, a doctor . . . a millionaire.' Believe me when I tell you this; I know people who are tired of being millionaires. It doesn't speak to their hearts. It's only a different kind of *shmeck taback*.

"In this world, what counts is what a person does for his true self. The Torah and *mitzvos* are lasting and fulfilling No one can take away from you your good deeds, or your learning. Being a Torah person, or a model of character lasts forever."

※ ※ ※

"Recently, I heard a speech at a ceremony for the conclusion of a volume of Talmud *(Yevamos)*. There, a young man stated that if someone offered him a million dollars for his year of learning he would turn it down flat. He had suffered too much to acquire that learning. Now I know that learning Talmud is very dear, but a million dollars?

"My dear friends, there is no comparison. For that young man Talmud is part of his soul. Compared to a piece of Talmud, a million dollars is just a *shmeck taback*."

The Last Rabbi Wein Story

I asked Rabbi Wein "When is an author finished working on his book? He answered with a hint of a smile, "When they rip it out of your hands." *So be it!*